T0161540

COMING EVENTS

(Collected Writings)

Susan Gevirtz

◇◇◇

NIGHTBOAT BOOKS
CALLICOON, NEW YORK

© 2013 Susan Gevirtz
Foreword © 2013 George Albon
All rights reserved
Printed in the United States

ISBN: 978-1-937658-08-3

Design and typesetting by Margaret Tedesco
Text set in Goudy Old Style
Cover: ITC Officina Sans

Cataloging-in-publication data is available
from the Library of Congress

Distributed by the University Press of New England
One Court Street
Lebanon, NH 03766
www.upne.com

Nightboat Books
Callicoon, New York
www.nightboat.org

Cover image wrap:
Luc Deleu & T.O.P. Office (www.topoffice.to)
Construction X, 1994.
9 shipping containers, Arthur's Quay Park, Limerick City
As part of EV+A 94, curated by Jan Hoet
(www.eva.ie)

To the memory of Barbara Guest
and "our" Dorothy Richardson

CONTENTS

ACKNOWLEDGEMENTS

The work collected in *Coming Events* represents an ongoing attempt to participate in a world including and beyond the market list and other necessities of daily survival. The hope has always been that a conversation (even if not direct) might occur or continue. Since the work here spans twenty one years it is impossible to name the many who have made this work possible. But I have deepest gratitude for all of them and to the editors who have published this work.

Coming Events couldn't have come into being without the support and imaginative, incisive reading and re-reading of Steve Dickison. Gratitude beyond words to him. Gratitude also to Stephen Motika who thought that these writings should again see the light of day. Thanks also to Vivian Bobka, intrepid editor. And to Margaret Tedesco for continuous rich conversation, collaboration, and now design. Also to Clio, Carrie, and my whole family without whose presence and support this work would not have been possible.

Many of the pieces in *Coming Events* have been published previously, often in earlier versions. Detailed publication credits appear in the "Notes" section. Grateful thanks to the editors of these journals, magazines, and anthologies.

Other Light, Larger Sight: Susan Gevirtz's *Coming Events*

As though to signal that the last door of the house is the first door to the outside, Susan Gevirtz's final essay here is an "outer event," and quotes Robert Duncan.

> Ultimately, the good reason of our refusal to censor or to "correct" is that we seek not to get rid of what embarrasses us or what does not seem true to our lights but to go beyond embarrassment—beyond shame or disgust or outrage—to imagine in an other light, to see in a larger sight what we had rather was dismissed from view.

This lengthy preface from the 1972 version of *Caesar's Gate* is an example of just the "larger sight" Duncan advocates. This *Caesar's Gate*, coming seventeen years after the first one, is an advance on the (already intransigent) Divers Press original. That earlier book's handful of handwritten poems (among others normatively set) has now taken over; standard typesetting has been abolished in favor of Duncan's runic-looking cursive and the cold but versatile faces of the IBM Selectric. The slick glossy paper of the 1972 version facilitates reproduction of Jess's marvelous paste-ups (seven more than before) and at the same time further distantiates (while further personalizing) the production. Aside from the fact that it's bound, and reads from left to right, no trace of the conventional remains.

The presentation-not-mine having been erased, and the biblio-environment recast in one's own idiomatic terms, the speaker is now ready to receive.

WHAT IS IT YOU HAVE COME TO TELL ME?

Like a child going from her first paragraph to her second, or the clairvoyant encountering a sentry, or the initiate ready to take the next step, reception is the unconsciously right next step, even toward the bracingly new: the trails lead as soon as they appear.

Elsewhere in these pages, Susan Gevirtz describes the writing of Barbara Guest as *an interrogation of the structures of making, of meaning, and of the conduct of the writer in writing, toward language.* This testifying is an appropriate description of her own sense of task. The word "conduct" in particular reaches out. The pull of energies toward a central attractor, conduct is the grace-form of experience. (The shaded further meaning of poise is not irrelevant here.) Proper conduct properly conducts. It is simultaneously an attracting charge and the preparedness to greet it.

Among the among: The child's fraught relationship with learning, and the adult's with pedagogy; the Doctor Editor, the monster of authority who midwifes poems and diagnoses the feminine creator; film-light, technically elaborate and psychically intangible, as oneiric cousin to writing; the velocity-accident as calibrator of forward life, among injured and unscathed; reports from the boiler rooms of multi-language symposia from a "voyeur of translation;" the vexed subject of discursive writing, bane and seduction—the thrown discus landing where it will, but even then with the tendency to orient discourse; and far from least, the Candide's progress of a young woman writer among elders, women writers, who offered (and offer) support, dialogues, and challenge.

What is at stake is the search for the third. For the exigency that comes to *bear*, not as a mean between two points, but from the scatter filling in from the antinomies.

Genres not as such but as weaves of instinct and intention. As an individual's stubborn writing angle showing through the cultural pressure. And revealed by attention to the intermediate, to the musculature, the lacings, that separate core from surface. "Three desks." In this case, one for dissertation writing, and one at the side, "for writing related to the topic of the dissertation but occurring in an idiolect different from that of the academy. What I recognized as poetry, sometimes related to the dissertation topics and sometimes not, fell to the third table behind me." So does writing make claim to right-angled application *and* eccentric space. (One poet, in the days before PCs, kept a manual typewriter in every room of the house, a different poem "going" in each one.)

And the occasions when the investigation is pitched so forwardly, so searchingly, that it must break into single words, isolated phrases—not a release of tension but its logical maintenance, "a place is a disturbance that has been claimed."

Of her pioneer work on the near-occluded career of Dorothy Richardson, offshoots have made their way inside here. It's tantalizing to speculate how many readers will experience their first sustained introduction to this exemplary *tertium quid* writer (it was thus for myself), and proceed to undertake the *Pilgrimage*.

Wonder-as-first-order is a place owned by children, only rented out past childhood by vocation. After the secret garden, it is a taxing and obdurate process of self-initiation, self-motivation, and other-immersion. "The conditions," she writes, "funnel certain necessary kinds and orders of speech. Is that what gets separated at birth and then fashioned into myth or argument?" And it's a process from which radical uncertainty is never absent. Close by are concerns over habits and practices we use to get through the day, and then let slip into the hermeneutic project, where they should be faced down, or at least given careful scrutiny. Watchfulness like this is a torsion, but necessary in order to burn a hole through borrowed thought and gain access to the crucial instrument, Oppen's "mind which searches for terms." The rewards are ongoing rather than conclusive, and these pieces at their best both situate and extend. The "way" of them is *way*—pathmarks lit by an intensive. In their refusal of capsule treatment, in their embrace of difficult discriminations, in their respect for care-taking, and their sensuous connectivity, they embolden their readers, who feel here the *conduct* toward a spectrum of particularly won intellective-affective tones—the true pitch of an erotics of study.

—GEORGE ALBON

COMING EVENTS

◇◇◇◇◇◇◇

THREE DESKS

My Little Read Backwards Book

When the mother interrupts the small child while she is deeply engrossed in play, the child learns to interrupt herself.

Speak between lines a talk that may not *not* escape its breasted body either, nor its lambasted psyche sinking to the floor—No. Offspring, what we ask of you is reverse comfort tactics. Engastriloquy. Once I spoke with the birds. After the trees shut up no grammars have caught me. Speech rising. Cunt stomach throat up through the trunk. But cancelled early. First grade was the first fire retardant. They snuffed them out all at once. A whole room of us bound tidily at our desks. I saw us attempt to comply, most too young to sit still for long. I saw that there were codes escaping me again. They were in numbers and manners. The tone of instruction telegraphed punishment first. Then maybe reward, never understanding. I could see that there would be consequences but wasn't clear on their nature. Something to do with 'leave the room and stay in it at the same time.' Institution starts early and stays in some like a badge of honor. Stays on others like an encounter with a skunk. But stays.

A small breakdown. Undetectable to others maybe. A processing glitch in the brain. A perception error of the emotional landscape.

A deprivation chamber can only seem to be one if there is something else to compare it to. There was a school where dinosaur bones could be found in a sandbox.

In exile or just an idiot. Flummoxed. Distressed. Regressed. And so reversion to language before and during trauma. Before and after drama of this public.

Tossed and turned all night. Which dys- is it keeping me awake? Phoria? Lexia? Topia? Gather around daughters and I will tell you a story.

    Debasement, my familiar

    come sit on my right

Come to me again

let me feel

the usual

Done what I can with what was given. Was inborn. What more?

So it goes after another exposure to the academic—to which I remain allergic. Even the buildings as I enter a campus. Like the driveway where I approach that I may say something wrong. Or the dinner table where no voice but one can be heard.

There was suddenly a hard rain in the night and I was up for the duration.

It is not only my driveway or dinner table. Not only my night, my rain, my sense that's there's something awry in the belfry that tolls hourly: "what distinguishes philosophy from mythology is generally thought to be the presence of arguments supporting its assertions."[1] There is nothing to argue or assert. Mythology and philosophy have not yet banished the propositions of poetry. Imagining or remembering a time but not exactly in nostalgia— more a time parallel to the time of trauma—a time sustained against the broken time of interruption. The conditions funnel certain necessary kinds and orders of speech. Is that what gets separated at birth and then fashioned into myth or argument?

The situation of disturbance or idiocy I am describing, that occurs after the separation, the interruption, is a martial situation which requires a response.

Gather round and I will tell you a story of distrust of story but reliance on story as it was all that was available, and sometimes is all that is available. Distrust of story because it makes a case for itself, not because of its linear progression. Things are not where I left them, "the crooked way"—so this becomes more a following of crumbs left by

Little Jewish girl of the '50s drinking from the well of *My Little Red, Green* and *Blue Story Books*:

> Susan said, "Father! Betty!
> See the funny airplane.
> See the funny, funny airplane!"
>
> Tom said, "See Susan go."
> See Susan and Father.
> See the airplane go up and down.

Then, at about twelve-years-old, inventing a way to teach those younger than me, having difficulties reading, how to read backwards. First I'd record them telling a story. Then they wrote down their story while listening to the transcript of their own voice. Then adjusted the order of the telling if it needed adjusting, and made pictures to go with it. Then they read this book back to me aloud as I recorded them. Then I played the recording of them reading their story back to them…. Oddly this worked pretty well. Maybe I then continued to teach as a kind of reparation for having been dis-taught. And maybe as a stopgap for future not-yet-happened disaster-traumas like mine that could visit, or may have already visited, others.

Figment of Appointment

IPSUM YAHODO VITCH

CAPSCUM RUSCHA

OMERO ONADO O-C-A-L-Y-ROTA

By Every Different Means

On leaf On counter On tire

Amorous antennae luphibius ancestor

Your Color cognations Sing Sing Sung

Of when Before it was no longer necessary

it was once again Or Else

telephonic insomnia:
and no choice remained but to take notes

CAPELERIA ENCAPSULATE WINNOW

TUNDRAROAD

vast expense conversant

It's like them to say finally, tenderly—
as the sun falls again into the vast maw of sea—

    "adorable impediment

    conversant impediment"

Homare Osage Recid

    CHEVROLET

    CADILLAC

    CHILDHOOD

    Hang your head over
    Hear the great plains below

By the time I got to Sacramento I realized
someone had been in the car all along

I promised I would read to you so bring popcorn and curl up

    Schlassa impregnatiously ota timeaus
    upona equaynation and out they went

Don't give me that expression   it's never been my fault that tea gets cold   hold out your
hand tenacious listenophonia

warm by the hearth
while out in the storm they unpack the trunk
it is not your job to call the home insurance company
curl and strike
while I hover over dispensing feather

Pull up a ledge and feed your view
It is a pet you can always count on to talk back
Invotoritia recorum ipsulantova tecusa lets inten and rows and rows of hedge-weeks wait
for a quorum. Or:
Freedonis teraban, come in come in calafirm.
Translation no longer necessary
if you listen in vorasimilitude

Oh wandering little ovation
Let me supply you with a nest
nothing fancy just one parking place
in a bed where you can meet your match
wrestle squabble tease resist

I do not OVERCALIBRATE your valumificance
instead hush huss sing sing and sung along to the land where
breakfast is not yet ready
The kings oh die in the arms of your throngs
The ponds oh suck long tresselites of the choked
limpid on still waters above
yet we do not hungerflack for era
nor wist for farflung bardelodium
the drowned the drowned they will drone on

We of phobic diagnosis
ears gathered not for recitation
but do repeat
someone had been along
all along

◊◊◊◊◊◊◊

On the night after the day I was asked to participate in this series I fell asleep and
had a dream all in the other language above. At the end of the dream the words
"TRANSLATION IS NO LONGER NECESSARY" appeared as if on a dark billboard.
After all, I had thought during the day while awake, what is there to say *about* the work,
that hasn't already been said *in* the work?

◊◊◊◊◊◊◊

The furniture's arrangement equals induction. Between commas, the summons.

She entered as punctuation: "For language as it conforms to rule and punctuation is
invisible," says Dorothy Richardson in her 1924 essay "About Punctuation."[1] "About
Punctuation" begins: "Only to patient reading will come forth the charm concealed in
ancient manuscripts. Deep interest there must be, or sheer necessity, to keep eye and brain
at their task of scanning a text that moves unbroken, save by an occasional full-stop."
It was necessary to work at three desks at once in order to evade what Richardson calls the
punctuation "police." Necessary because on the computer screen the "formal law" glared.
"The formal law," says Richardson, "was strictly observed only by scholars. Not until lately
have infringements, by the ordinary, been regarded as signs of ill breeding. And in high
places there have always been those who honored the rules in breech without rebuke."[2]

At one desk a poem:

"Romansh: the stations of canonization"[3]

We have nothing but
second languages

as if there is home
travel

You are in a foreign place
when your own name
is unrecognizable.

give up easily

in prophecy

up folds
time

We are on location
You are ballast
in a state of readiness

"In what room will they put
me to forget them?"

The useful dead
drink the sun
down into the ocean

illegal removal
sale or cutting up of
the hour of our

nothing of the soft tissue
holy intentions
davor davor
left "the seduction of having oneself
dismembered alive
for others"

perforate incognito
blaspheme to make more

In which
second language

shall we stop
to forget them?

                preserve mystery her
amnesiac assimilation

        "concupiscence" or the formation of adipocere
        thauma
        turge id ead

        ideas rampant on shore

On the computer screen a conference paper:

"Recreative Delights and Spiritual Exercise: Pantheism As Aesthetic Practice in Dorothy Richardson's Pilgrimage"[4]

> If only she could make Eve see what a book was… a dance by the author, a song, a prayer, an important sermon, a message. Books were not stories printed on paper, they were people; the real people.

—Dorothy Richardson, *Honeycomb*[5]

In a 1923 review of Dorothy Richardson's *Revolving Lights*, Virginia Woolf referred to herself as an "intermittent student" of Richardson's.[6] Later in the same review Woolf coined the phrase, "the psychological sentence of the feminine gender," to describe Richardson's style. In Richardson's techniques Woolf heard what she called "the damned egotistical self" while others simply found the work too difficult to read or boring. However, some readers, such as critic Louise Morgan, recognized (in 1931) that Richardson was doing "something entirely new with the English language." [7]

May Sinclair was one of the first to use William James' term "stream of consciousness," a term Richardson disliked, in a review of the three novel-chapters which open *Pilgrimage*:

> To me these three novels show an art and method and form carried to punctilious perfection…. In this series there is no drama, no situation, no set scenes. Nothing happens. It is just life going on and on.
>
> …In identifying herself with this life, which is Miriam's stream of consciousness, Miss Richardson produces her effect of being the first, of getting closer to reality than any of our novelists who are trying so desperately to get close.[8]

In 1925 Woolf said that, "If a writer… could write what he chose… there would be no plot, no comedy, no tragedy, no love interest or catastrophe in the accepted style."[9] The ideal novel in which "nothing happens" is the one Richardson attempted to write.[10] Richardson speaks of a "growing conviction that the extraneous matter was more essential than the interesting deliberately composed narrative, incidents and figures."[11] Writing was her means of addressing the way in which she was "perpetually haunted by the mutability of ideas. Giving no satisfaction to a growing desire to express the immutable."[12]

Richardson writes always in the vicinity of her mother's death, as if hovering around a shrine. The death itself is never directly mentioned in *Pilgrimage*, through her writing Richardson is able to approach it without entirely merging with it—without actually committing suicide or dying herself. She thereby fills the corporate silence with the "miracle" of "messages" from the womb/tomb of the death she only barely missed preventing.

Richardson's "spiritual exercise" and Miriam's journey towards writing constitute an approach and avoidance of the dead mother…. Travel towards the mother also occurs in this kind of collapsed or cinematic time in which one writes in what Richardson calls a "real dream" while one is simultaneously awake in "the real part of… life." The "feminine equivalent" is, in this sense, a vehicle not only for writing outside of the constraints of linear time and linear syntax, but also a vehicle for unconscious travel:

> that idea of visiting places in dreams. It was something more than that…. all the real part of your life has a real dream in it; some of the real dream part of

you coming true. You know in advance when you are really following your life. These things are familiar because reality is here. Coming events cast *light*. It is like dropping everything and walking backwards to something you know is there.

—Dorothy Richardson, *The Tunnel*[13]

The places in *Pilgrimage* where the written message becomes dream, music, or prayer epitomize that wavering border between sense and nonsense, speech and silence—the corporate silence of death and the incorporate speech of life. These moments are best exemplified on the page by narrative disruptions achieved through a deep engagement with what she refers to as the "contemplative state" of "feminine prose." The words break down or dissolve into music and the blank spaces on the page give way to that which is "all too sacred for words," the "nothing" which generates "meaning" even if "you have just murdered someone," or even if someone has just murdered herself and you feel responsible. Thus, the nerves of Richardson's practice exist where the writing wavers between word and ideogram, embodying a "habit of ignoring, while writing, the lesser of the stereotyped system of signs" and a "small unconscious departure from current usage."[14] In *March Moonlight*, the last of the novel-chapters, Miriam describes these irrevocable links between the written word, the sacred, and the "nothingness" of death:

To write is to forsake life. Every time I know this in advance. Yet whenever something comes that sets the tips of my fingers tingling to record it, I forget the price; eagerly face the strange journey down and down to the centre of being. And the scene of labour, when again I am back in it, alone, has become a sacred place.

—Dorothy Richardson, *March Moonlight*[15]

〈XXXXXXX〉

Next to the computer neither a poem nor an essay:

"Dorothy Richardson Taken Place"[16]

To write is to forsake life. Every time I know this in advance. Yet whenever
something comes that sets the tips of my fingers tingling to record it, I forget the
price; eagerly face the strange journey down and down to the centre of being. And
the scene of labour, when again I am back in it, alone, has become a sacred place.

—Dorothy Richardson, *March Moonlight*

Words mark vicinities where is the absence of a person. That absence we're after. Every
death sacrifice. We know because we haven't died and those invisible, having done that
for us, beckon down Where you Were you were constant in absence

alone, has become

a sacred place

Dorothy Richardson donated her body to the Royal College of Physicians and Surgeons
before her death. More than two years after her death, what remained was buried under
a tombstone inscribed "To the Memory of Dorothy Miriam Odle, Authoress D.M.
Richardson." Odle is the last name of Richardson's, by then dead, husband—a name
she almost never used in life. Miriam is the name of the main character in Richardson's
autobiographical thirteen volume epic novel *Pilgrimage*. The 'Miriam' on the tombstone
was a "mistake." No one knows who was responsible for it. Dorothy's actual middle name
was her mother's maiden name: Miller. Her mother's first name was Mary. In *Pilgrimage*
Miriam's mother is only called Mrs. Henderson.

Due to the lapse in time between Richardson's death and burial, the location of her grave
cannot be determined by the date of her death. In the cemetery records her name appears

17

in the later period of time when Streatham Park received her body. There is no other legal record. The temporary gap between death and interment, document and event, throws into disarray the usual correspondence between site and time. A disarray that unfolds the careful origami of identity: no meeting at the handshake of date—space—salutation

Name is a disturbance of place

"in many languages the word used for 'writing' is derived from verbs meaning 'to paint,' 'to cut,' 'to incise' or 'to scratch.'"[17] At fifty-two Mary Richardson slit her throat with a kitchen knife while twenty-two year old Dorothy was out for a brief walk. *To write is to forsake life*:

> Lodgings were rented at 11 Devonshire Terrace in Hastings, and Dorothy and her mother arrived there late in November, 1895. The sea was rough, the air somewhat cool, but after a few days Dorothy thought her mother looked better. She did not leave her alone for a moment. There was always something her mother needed done for her or something she wanted to try to express. At night Mary Richardson found it hard to sleep. Dorothy heard her moans and tried to reassure her: she was not stupid, she was not sinful, she was not eternally damned. Dorothy wanted desperately to convince her mother of all this, but Mary Richardson had accumulated nearly thirty years of evidence to the contrary. And precisely because her husband would have found it incontrovertible proof of her stupidity that she believed in damnation, she was absolutely certain of both. Dorothy herself wanted to cry out in loathing and anguish. Instead she went out one morning to escape. It was Saturday November 30. Hastings was quiet, the season long over. Dorothy wandered about for an hour or so, hoping to still the pounding in her head and erase from her mind's eye the image of self-loathing that was her mother's entire being, hoping she would not herself go mad. When she got back to Devonshire Terrace, her mother was dead. Somehow she had laid her hands upon a kitchen knife and cut her throat with it.
>
> —Gloria Fromm[18]

A place is a piece of the whole environment that has been claimed by feelings.

—A. Gussow [19]

The situation is the one in which a certain disturbance of the person occurs…
a seism which causes knowledge or the subject to vacillate: it creates *an emptiness
of language*.

—Roland Barthes[20]

To be awake in dreamtime is to be the audience in cinematic time. At once in the past,
present and future. Travel towards the mother also occurs in this collapsed time in which
she writes in a "real dream" while simultaneously awake in "the real part of your life."

In name disturbed place
walks toward
memory

The who in the dream I write to you about is all who but through them each lives a
cordoned one

The "spiritual exercise" writes the wounds of the lacerated body into the work of the
living. Providing her dead mother with an ulterior eternal life and death in the book she
gives herself a subterfuge for the past which continues as she writes.

Where is the state of the living

Writing that gives the absent other voice and flesh occurs where delivery and reception
blend, opening an equivalent gate to heaven and eternal damnation:

Some kind of calculation is at work, a sort of spiritual metronome, imperceptible
save when something goes wrong. It operates, too, upon sentences. A syllable too
many or a syllable too few brings discomfort, forcing one to make an alteration;
even if the words already written are satisfactory. Perhaps everyone has a definite
thought-rhythm and speech-rhythm, which cannot be violated without producing

self-consciousness and discomfort?

      The whole process is strange. Strange and secret, always the same, always a mystery and an absence from which one returns to find life a little further on…. To open the book is to begin life anew, with eternity in hand.

          —Dorothy Richardson, *Clear Horizon*

Imperceptible save when something goes wrong on paper print vacillates. Thought-rhythm and speech-rhythm: figment of appointment.

A place is a disturbance that has been claimed
Small metronome on wrist of departure

Pieces of her
body remain

in science silence

      Sound exists only while it is going out of existence.

          —Walter Ong

Monogram at the lapse
of landscape

In addition to the
dead
the injured
in addition to
the injured the
newborn
unborn and those
caught in destinies not
their own
in addition to the owned,
the made
followed by
the counted

Richardson's choice of words and names is too precise, as Stephen Heath suggests, for it to be accidental that embedded in the name *Miriam* is the possibility of "Mirror I am" and that Miriam is linked by sound to the word *myriad*. The name reflects Richardson's preoccupation with themes of feminine subjectivity present throughout her writing.

The study of what becomes visible and who is heard in the land of rebuke becomes the only game in town. But hearing doesn't happen nowhere. Richardson leads us away from the domestic in the only escape vehicle available to women before the turn-of-the-century, the pilgrimage. And *at* the turn-of-the century, the film. On pilgrimage to the shrine of the cinema, having escaped a "shrill London afternoon," is where, she says, you will find a whole "new audience" of "Tired women" taking "sanctuary."[21]

And, if a member of this audience turns her head away from the screen, what Richardson calls the "white searchlight" of the projector, will reveal the spectacle of female spectators in the act of viewing. Here, in the moment of turning away, Richardson's film writing begins. Are the spectators guilty, she asks—caught in the private act of reading—what she calls "the unpunished vice"—in public? Under the electric light, invented in 1879, about seventeen years before the first experiments in cinema, and six years after Richardson was born, night could suddenly become day, images and text could hover in a twilight state suggesting contemplation and decipherment as acts that might expose the reader to herself. As does Miriam in *Pilgrimage*, Richardson breaks convention by living alone and writing after work under her own rented electric light. What appeared as she turned the beam on the apparition of herself by herself? As Richardson describes Miriam in *Pilgrimage*[22]:

> Returning from scribbling in various styles of handwriting the difficult combination, she gazed once more at the word on the page and saw that as written by the girl it was not a word at all. It was a picture, a hieroglyph, each letter lovely in itself....
>
> Written as she wrote it, it was expressive exactly as her script was expressive: a balance of angles and curves. Like the words traced on the mirror.[23]

> —Dorothy Richardson, *Dawn's Left Hand*[24]

It is here in this mirror light, under a bushel of light, that I beheld her, myself in the act of crime: impudent girl behind a closed door watching herself read, or was that touching herself?

"Nymphae! Vestibulum! Words that could only be derived from the knowledge of books!" says Freud—accusing her of secret reading—when Dora utters them.[25]

Freud: "I informed Dora of the conclusions I had reached. The impression made upon her must have been forcible, for there immediately appeared a piece of the dream which had been forgotten: in it "She went calmly to her room and began reading a big book that lay on her writing table."[26]

I saw myself I saw Miriam doing what Freud said Dora did—Richardson rewriting, while simultaneously in another city, Freud was writing. I turned the beam back, I bent it. I scanned what I saw—a text that moves unbroken—at once film frame and ancient manuscript. Here she entered as deep interest, sheer necessity, the sight of the word

How sleepless is the air.

I went into my room and closed the door. For twenty years. Acts that might expose the reader to herself. Alone I was summoned to account. In this vestibule we stand accused. Speak and be breast, be beast— What does writing have to do with our mothers? Wear her body's doubt—inherit—reveal the word for the writing implement. In the academy of the daily every word we utter becomes anatomy. Stand at the entrance to your forest and condemn yourself by vocabulary, vestibulary. When the parents closed the door for the final time I use to get up and rearrange the furniture before going to sleep. I tried to reassure her, she was not stupid, she was not sinful…

We always return to the scene of the crime. There is nowhere else to go. Nowhere else we want to go. Is it an airplane or theatre? Operating room or kitchen? Like a big cloak dropped from ten stories above light billows out, falls over the shoulders of the audience turning them to landscape. Sleep, like a big x-ray apron weights us   As I turned away, there, immediately, appeared a piece of dream:

Prosthesis[27]

Without name there is less to forget
Where the fathers are ashes in the mouth of
the future Where in that bend of the road they still
crouch knitting and rubbing in an attempt at sense

in the gentle and long the impossible
bandaging of themselves

Dear ventriloquist,

This uncertainty in regard to direction—For which
    they are either drowned or burned—
Engastriloques, under the trees—Talking to birds—To which
we reply

Dorothy Richardson Taken Place

Damnation mirror
ere

Disturbance	[the ancestor dies]
Memorial	[and to this present day a circle of stones marks the spot]
Event	[landscape is made out of the activity of those who are no longer seen]
Incident	[in India… each temple is built over a portion of the fallen and dismembered body of a deity]
Distribution	of the pieces = locales

only here not there

[There is nothing in the temple but the tabernacle; there is nothing in the tabernacle]

> There was no thought in the silence, no past or future, nothing but the strange thing for which there were no words, something that was always there as if by appointment, waiting for one to get through to it away from everything in life. It was the thing that was nothing. Yet it seemed the only thing that came near and meant anything at all. It was happiness and realization. It was being suspended, in nothing. It came out of oneself because it came only when one had been a long time alone. It was not oneself. It could not be God. It did not mind what you were or what you had done. It would be there if you had just murdered someone.
>
> —Dorothy Richardson, *Interim*

It came out of oneself. *It* was not oneself. *It* could not be God. It would be *there*.

> If one were perfectly still the sense of God was there. Things were astounding enough; enough to make you die of astonishment, if you did nothing at all. Being *alive*. If one could realize that clearly enough, one *would* die. Everything one did was just a distraction from astonishment.
>
> —Dorothy Richardson, *Honeycomb*

25

The Quakers, with whom Richardson had a long association, believe that in order to commune with "the beyond that is within," with "corporate silence," or what Richardson calls "the strange thing for which there were no words," it is necessary to empty oneself and become like "a hollow tube."[1] One's body is then a conduit for the "message." Emptying was an act that, as Richardson put it, required "fierce concentration." The avenue directly into death by astonishment. She uses this technique in the writing of what she calls "feminine prose." This notion of the body as source of message begins to address why for Richardson the spiritual is so closely allied to the aesthetic, and how the disturbance of a stable subject is necessary to the technique of "feminine" writing. In her terms the empty, wordless and disturbed all meet in post-Victorian "feminine" consciousness: a state of aesthetic that, she believed, allied women more closely to the "being at the heart of all becoming," while men were busy becoming something.

In the same way that a pilgrim might have treated the fingernail clippings of a saint, Miriam, who like Dorothy becomes a writer in the course of *Pilgrimage*, fetishizes both the book and the word as relic, charm, amulet. Writing itself, practiced according to the ritual of "fierce concentration," is the vehicle by which relics can be produced and linguistic shrines approached. In the context of their belief in language as animate, certain words become sacred because, like charms and amulets, they are remnants of, or "messages" from an original holy body. Emanating from an original body these "messages" of silence simultaneously invoke the end of a story, of a life and the promise lodged in the impossibility of ending because: "Being *alive*. If one could realize that clearly enough, one *would* die." The shrine of the "beyond that is within," a womb and tomb, summons, in its doubleness, the cave-like niches in medieval shrines where pilgrims curled up in fetal position while praying for cures. If one could get close enough one would die.

Charms that were condemned by the church of the Middle Ages as a form of magic (as opposed to a form of religion) were often written down and then placed on a patient's body. Sometimes miracles were written on parchment and bound to an ailing person. In the early twentieth century in parts of France it was believed that tooth ache could be relieved by touching the sore gum with a piece of paper on which a prayer was written. The fourth book of the *Iliad* used to be placed under the pillow to cure ague, but in twelfth century England the Gospel of John or a relic was used. A third century Roman doctor recommended writing abracadabra repeatedly on parchment, which was folded up and carried around in the pocket of a good Christian.[2] The interchangeability between the Gospel of John and a relic, a character and a conversation: physical proximity to writing could warm the hands. As a compilation of relics, written words substitute for the figment of an original cohesive body and voice. A circle of stones marks the spot—fierce ritual pays attention—seize a locale of worship.

Nothing shall have taken place but place.

—Stéphane Mallarmé, *Un coup de dés…*[3]

To carry the word abracadabra in a pocket is not far from Miriam's belief that a book is "a dance by the author, a song, a prayer, an important sermon, a message." Not far from her statement that "Books were not stories printed on paper, they were people; the real people…." As a "real" person a book, like an enshrined saint, does not move or speak, though through the figment of an author it has spoken, and having spoken retains the promise as possibility of future speech. To read is future speech channeled by substitution through someone else's mouth.

When who disturbs there

Hovering at a shrine in the vicinity of her Mother's death. Though *Pilgrimage* is highly autobiographical, the death of Miriam's and Dorothy's mother is never directly mentioned. It is hinted at in the end of *Honeycomb* and marked by a rectangular blank space where a thin paragraph could fit.[4] Through the forsaking of life that is writing, Dorothy and Miriam join Mary. Merge with the dead without dying. They fill corporate silence with the "miracle" of messages from the site of the death they only missed preventing by the brevity of a walk.

Without Event: The Reign Of Commotion

The observer infects the observed with his own mobility.

—Samuel Beckett, *Proust and Three Dialogues*

Thus the interrogation of the mode of mobility

Sojourn

Ida came over first with her sons. Then they sent for her husband and their daughter. After the long sea voyage, they were turned away at immigration in New York. The officers called the daughter retarded and said she was forbidden to enter the United States. Sam and his daughter returned to Russia. "As a little girl, I had always wondered," said *my* grandmother, "why my grandmother was so depressed. When I was older I found out that it was because she never saw her husband or child again."

> Or rather life is a succession of habits, since the individual is a succession of individuals; the world being a projection of the individual's consciousness... the pact must be continually renewed, the letter of safe conduct brought up to date. The creation of the world did not take place once and for all time, but takes place every day.
>
> —Beckett

Not once and for all time
Now past now present now future

Sojourn

It was 1920. After a weekend jaunt down south, they were heading back home to Cleveland through a blizzard. Cousins were packed into the car. Skidding around a bend, the door flew open. Esther was propelled out into the snow and died on the roadside.

> He is present at his own absence. And, in consequence of his journey and his anxiety, his habit is in abeyance....
>
> —Beckett

Every day habits of thinking are modes of mobility

CATALOGUE: *Accidents*

A way of remembering thinking
A way of remembering is thinking

Memory is the momentum by which
the succession of days is renewed

    form is the fossil
    memory path
    of ratiocination
    hit the page

He is present at his own accident

> It should be illegal to publish a book by a man without
> a woman first annotating it.
>
> —Dorothy Richardson, *Deadlock*

She recalls her own absence before and after it has happened as if present in, as if
conveyance of collision

Commotion:

> The element of memory was a perfectly feasible thing, so then I gave it up. I then
> started a book which I called A Long Gay Book to see if I could work the thing up
> to a faster tempo. I wanted to see if I could make that a more complete vision. I
> wanted to see if I could hold it in the frame.
>
> —Gertrude Stein, "How Writing Is Written"

How the film frame is a window of tempo…
Without frame to where does panorama pass?

Railway accidents produced "a commotion so extreme as to blot out memory."

—Wolfgang Schivelbusch, *The Railway Journey*
(*all unattributed information and quotes in the text are from this source*)

"…There is something in the crash, the shock…"

"Immediately after the accident the victim felt completely normal; after one or two days he became overwhelmed by the memory of the event. Their effects are immediate and remote."

No events: only a purely physical sense

Charles Dickens, after a minor railroad accident on June 9, 1865, from which he escaped entirely unscathed, says in a letter four days later:

> I don't want to be examined at the inquest and I don't want to write about it.
> I could do no good either way, and I could only seem to speak about it to
> myself…. I am keeping very quiet here. I have a—I don't know what to call it—
> constitutional (I suppose) presence of mind, and was not in the least fluttered
> at the time. I instantly remembered that I had the MS of a number with me
> and clambered back into the carriage for it. But in writing these scanty words
> of recollection I feel the shake and I am obliged to stop. Ever faithfully,
> Charles Dickens.
>
> —(quoted in Schivelbusch)

I don't want to be examined. I don't want to write. VERY QUIETLY I don't know what to call it and I instantly remembered, immediate and remote—I don't know what—and am obliged to stop.

A revulsion takes place, he bursts into tears... there is a sense of alarm

Velocity:

> One thing which came to me is that the Twentieth Century gives of itself a feeling of movement, and has in its way no feeling for events.

—Stein

In 1866: Three works simultaneously presented in medical journals report on the specific nature of the railroad accident:

> This kind of accident did not differ from other accidents in principle but in the degree of violence, with the additional observation that the degree was a new and previously unknown one. Subsequently that observation proved to be the great contradiction with which the medical authors tried to come to terms.

There is something in the crash, the shock "...and the violence of a railway collision, which would seem to produce effects upon the nervous system quite beyond those of any ordinary injury. In some cases, we are told, the sufferer may not even have sustained any fracture, and the cuts and external injuries may be apparently slight to the visual perception of the medical man; whilst notwithstanding the comparatively and apparently external trifling injury or injuries, yet there may be coincident with all this, such a *shock* to the system as for a time to shatter the whole constitution, and this moreover, to such a degree, to such an extent, that the unfortunate sufferer may not altogether recover throughout the remainder of his life, which I apprehend, may, in some instances at least, be reasonably expected to be curtailed in its duration."

—Schivelbusch

DEAR POSSIBLE

Dear possible, and if you drown,
Nothing is lost, unless my empty hands
Claim the conjectured corpse
Of empty water—a legal vengeance
On my own earnestness.

—Laura (Riding) Jackson

Motion beyond motion immeasurable   *if you drown*

A pile of sheaves has fallen

Catalogue: SHOCK

The history of shock, which is, in large measure, part of military history: shock was first adapted as a military term.

Shock—Germanic—a pile of sheaves.

—*Oxford English Dictionary*

From rider on horse to mass modern armies: One thousand deliver one blow when they charge

From craft to assembly line mode: the whole animal machine

Your specific state of readiness—vs—our general state of readiness

"The role of the hand firearms can be compared to the one played by the steam engine in the industrial revolution"

Perhaps the wound was not noticed at first, but every sensation requires a degree of attention, however small.

Now 'shock' describes the kind of sudden and powerful event of violence that disrupts the continuity of an artificially/mechanically created motion or situation, and also the subsequent state of derangement. The precondition for this is a highly developed general state of dominance over nature, both technically (military example: firearms) and psychically (military example: troop discipline). The degree of control over nature and the violence of the collapse of that control, in shock, are proportionate: the more finely meshed the web of mechanization, discipline, division of labor, etc., the more catastrophic the collapse when it is disrupted from within or without.

—Schivelbusch

Coded as nature, confined to the casualties of domesticity, was Victorian women's shock lodged in the loss of sons, fathers, husbands? Received as receipt of the collapse of his "control" over nature? Women in shock as perpetual symptom of his shock—as reminders of their collapse of control and confined for being perpetual memory of that. Hysteria as the alter-ego of shock spelled differently.

The accident of too much motion—or too little

In a new and previously unknown degree the possibility presents itself

Catalogue: STIGMATA

He met with his first accident. "I am weary of myself," he says. He passes through a period of passional attitudes. Animal bites appear on his arms.
A more important part in the genesis of these accidents than the wound itself is the terror experienced at the moment of the accident.
I pass before you figures
While his hands extended in vacancy he would clutch at some imaginary object

—Charcot, *Clinical Lectures*

Terrour   Terreur   Territory

The Ballad of Passion

the repetition of little terrors
that we'd kept up with

his confidence shall bring him to the
king of terrors   Kynge Terrour
our knight

or the most terrible of terrible

Hark guess   half guesses

The red, and the counter, white terror
Terror with hungry throat ravished the wide terrain

The stern throat of terror (Drayton, 1598)
curses all this terror-fraught interspace between

heaven and earth
haps and mishaps terror-tainted

—*O.E.D.*

Catalogue: Derailment, Velocity, Collisions, Upholstery

What at first seemed frightening became 'panoramic vision' and the 'novel activity of reading while travelling.'

Fear of derailment arising from the experience of travelling in what seemed like an enormous grenade, gave way to diversion—security based on familiarity—habit and the plush upholstery of later trains cushioned the vibrations and noise of train to track.

The traveler's psychic structure: the ability to ward off stimuli. The ability to forget the possibility of future experience.

Memory upholstery.

> All reification is forgetting: objects become mere things at the moment they are fixed without being actually present in all their parts—the moment when some part of them has been forgotten.
>
> —Adorno in a letter to Benjamin,
> 29 February 1940 (quoted in Schivelbusch)

"According to Reuleaux the progress of machine technology consists in the increasing elimination of *play*. Play signifies the relation of the elements of a machine to each other. The more primitive the technology, the less attuned the parts of the machine to each other, the greater the degree of play."

Forget the possibility of future experience

I anachronism writing as if I believe I recall something

Catalogue: Dismemberment—Fossil of Velocity in the late Twentieth Century

The available vehicles of representation alter the conditions of the imaginary. The conditions of imagination too represent the conditions of the imaginary itself. Also represents representation itself. The video monitor replaces the train window—what is the panorama of post-modern motion or situation?

Reorganized in the perpetual accident of the post-modern traveler's psychic structure. Immediate and remote. A personal memory

Learned to ask, "What is the worst thing that could happen?" And then to imagine that that thing had in fact occurred.

Catalogue: Memories

Voluntary
An instrument of reference
An instrument of discovery
Curiosity
Rememoration
Involuntary
Touristic
Memory that is not memory but application of concordance
Memory proper
Mere backward glance
Counter memory
Recovered memory
Random Access Memory
Cellular memory

—Recalled from Beckett, Foucault, Sloan, Richardson, Delp, Wright

⟨⟨⟨⟨⟨⟨⟨⟩

And of memory, suppressed memory, maybe And what about the mother of the muses? (Mnemosyne, if I remember.) Actual memory, repressed memory, desire to escape, desire to create (music), intellectual curiosity, a wish to make real to myself what is not real.

—H.D., "A Note on Poetry"

Autotopia

Autotopia is the name of a recurring dream and a ride at Disneyland.

The parents are in the front seat. The Father is driving. The child is in the back watching the road more carefully than either adult. They hurtle down a Los Angeles freeway at 75 miles-per-hour. The Father doesn't know how fast he is going. Suddenly both parents collapse on the front seats, dead. The child clambers quickly over the seat, and, pushing aside the corpse of her Father, takes the steering wheel in her hands. She knows how to drive as a result of the vigilant road watching she has done for years.

    Plans' hope
    Before the purple, blue, red
    bruised road

    driverless car
    small bumper cars, small drivers
    around the enclosed arena
    as if through a one way mirror
    a mistake corrected
            Tour detour
            our invisible track
            Rail
            bliss   the close
            collision

        steering world

both adult hands
here at end of
plans' curving road
without road

required to rescind
having foreseen end
future foresworn
territory already
past belonging

Catalogue: Recovered Memories: The Church of Living Waters

"Satan is real and walks the earth"

You will remember the abuse once you have confessed to it, said the police officers to each family member. And they did.

"Believe us!" demanded Ericka, the daughter.

The Minister: "There is an epidemic of Satanism in this country—not allegations."

Ericka and Julie (then twenty-two and eighteen respectively) charged their father with sexual molestation. Paul Ingram said that he could not ever remember molesting his daughters, but added, "If this did happen, we need to take care of it."

If you can imagine it, it happened—begin by looking off, as if through a window—

Paul Ingram, the father and a police officer, told of a past he saw. This sparked the dormant memories of his other children and wife. But, a year later, during the trial and while still in jail, "his memories began an insidious migration."

He said he had given incriminating testimony while in a trance-like state.

The visualizations of rituals and abuse had been fantasies, not actual memories. He no longer believed that he was a Satanist or a child abuser or even a victim of childhood abuse himself.

The two police officer-detectives, his former friends, sat in the back of the court and wept openly.

Whatever the true nature of human memory the Ingram case makes obvious the perils of a fixed idea—a curtain of amnesia over a painful past. Belief in repression is as dangerous as belief in witches.

All the stories were at war with each other.

—All information, quotes, and substantial
syntax sequences, from Lawrence Wright,
"Remembering Satan," *The New Yorker*

Sojourn

The degree of play had been eliminated. They sat in a movie therefore knowing what to do next. Predators were everywhere and the ability to say anything severely curtailed. Animal bites littered the sky.

Emigration

◇◇◇◇◇◇◇

ADDRESS

About "The One…" For Asher Montandon

There are degrees of being alive and sometimes I think the ones who are most alive are like searchlights at mall openings—the biggest brightest targets if you were a bomber roaming the sky. Or a gunner combing the streets of Los Angeles. Which is how he was put out.

A few weeks before he let the desperate man into the back seat, Asher wrote:

> I have read Hélène Cixous' "The Laugh of the Medusa" five times! It is my favorite thing to read. I am indulging in it as one does a new favorite album, listening over and over, finding nuances, figuring out the lyrics. It nourishes me. Her bodies sing me their 'unheard of songs.' There are parts I have read as many as ten times or so, out loud and silently, to others and to myself, for comprehension and pleasure.

But we live in a time of one false move. And that act—letting a man in terror, being chased, dive into the back seat—was his. The fact that the pursuer took immediate revenge on the driver, on him, is all of our fact.

Of what use was Cixous to him then? Why don't we teach in universities how to respond when someone points a gun at you? How to live in a city of hunger.

When I was told in second grade that one times one times one times one equals one, I remember knowing it wasn't true. One doesn't stand for one. Everyone is standing in for more. Every word broken off from a flock. It's the accident we all inhabit: "The world…" said Asher, "racing into the future like the Titanic into the North Atlantic, and those who looked ahead saw both shipwreck and the wonders of time travel." *

Put unheard of songs over him

(1992)

About About

Resuscitations

arm leg kindling gather where water blankets sound take her
down again again quiet crown

was strong singing heart you swimming practicing breathing
strip-mining the superfluous

to anything recalled ever to everything ever summoned the
former a project of the former

sea fence Sea Gate said promise of plenty said gather greens of
tomorrow mainland winds mountain up once every 4,200 seconds

from lucid sea like none ever witnessed abbreviation the
situation engineered a couldn't say (or far worse

and so tending to every and none seeing not saying bluntly a management
preoccupation in familiar waters

carefully considered beginning rests with the rest turning away
turns the turned

what is the meaning of the word *lagoon* what a tribute that you're
all still here sweet nothings

warm in flannel under the ground "here's what we'll do—
when you sleep I'll sleep, when you wake up I'll wake up"

a long way to Tipperary to the place by the ocean its fishermen
and fine sand see the crypt correcting herself

land owners want land boat owners want bones boats want shortwave sound
wants bait land lies in wait

someone was behind her also a man was near pointing "You're
still there" unable to name or swim panting

between finger and singer machine's refrain between teeth
the difference

crosshairs correcting the spiral of wandering attention's
gunscope once I arrived landscape's low status slow statues

of noise no promise longer than sea's sleep that never rests short
of words over over sent

stick figure swaddled in chain mail escape hatch unlocks picture postcards finger's
touch

by sea's preface before the world was faceless now her face take swallows silence
soon down

the word regret the word repent whiplash on halved horizon be-headed by halves
the almost left holds hope behind right's back

belies the way face belies fact an act to cover the desire for never achieved or
relation to idea as act

wound or sunken awoken profile proximity's imposition face on
face of

and at our last parting last words I promised enfolded routing in
the gulf offing

written in caterpillar scar constellation written in rain star launch reserves
literally last week's facsimile face used up

plenaria aria axis belief voids all attempts sent to preliminary
galaxy beyond belief's chair

When the phone rings and no one is there I say to my grandmother, "next time wait a little longer and we can speak." Absence of breath at the receiver. Because it conveys voice the phone is an instrument of breath. But the poem is not an instrument, it's an incident. It occurs at the moment of picking up the silent phone. The moment when the dead have just ceased to speak. And just begun to speak. And the newly born have not yet resorted to the inadequacy of words—having just come from worlds of far more subtle articulation. "For this moment, this death-in-life when our breath is taken away, yet turns and re-turns, Celan coins the word *Atemwende*."[1] The breath is clock. The breath makes reading hearing. What time is it? Time to listen for your life, that is, to write. "Sometimes we write... so as to name an age, the one that comes to us from our mother, sometimes to celebrate the natal event, and the author of the event, the mother."[2] Sometimes all authors fall away and writing writes the collision of events. Our breath is taken away.

It is true that Clio was born on April 6, 1997. And also true that my ninety-one year old grandmother died three weeks later. This three weeks was a 'turning of breath'—a lathe— in which an encounter occurred, a shape was presented.

My grandmother never met Clio but she saw pictures. I spoke to her on the phone a few hours after Clio was born. I called her often in the first weeks of Clio's life. In those weeks she was shuttling between many worlds but whenever I called she immediately and clearly said, "How is she?!"

The poem (as always) is About about. Which means that events were an environment of conversation, but the poem is not about events. The poem is about the impossibility of writing *about* events. In disguise as convoys for about, but actually serving only as decoys, since about is never actually possible, are the conventions of telling, of grammar, of reading from left to right, of story, etc.... After the necessary abolishment of these decoys from the land of the poem, after *about* falls away, only about about is left (only the decoys of the decoys are left).

At the same time that my grandmother was going and coming, Clio was trying to stay. As with many babies, her breathing was erratic. She was kept an extra day in the hospital for observation as she had apneia—uneven breathing with alarmingly long pauses between breaths. I had sat at my grandmother's bedside for ten days in January when she seemed to be dying. Her breath was also ragged. Sometimes she sounded like someone running, then the parched lips and rasp of great thirst, then nothing, next a half-smothered inhale, a sudden deep breath and back again to an uneven rhythm.

The sound of the story, the shadow of the story on the ground, displaces its small body, high up in a sky, getting smaller and farther away each time the phone rings.

One evening during that January bedside vigil when I was seven months pregnant, my grandmother said she heard a baby crying. I was not in the room. My sister told me to come in. I had recently read that at this stage of fetal development babies can cry in utero. I found this disturbing—how can you hear the crying? How can you comfort a baby who is crying inside? When I arrived in my grandmother's room my grandmother said, "Come here." She put one hand on my stomach and closed her eyes. Then she added the other hand. "Oh, she's crying, but she will be okay," she said, her eyes still closed. Then she said, "Sweet baby…" and began to hum, then "You will be lucky, you will have a wonderful life, you will be healthy, all will be well…." humming to the baby, patting my stomach.

Are you there? Either of you? "I see my invisible…. The thing that will come from us to us so as to escape us."[3]

After she died I dreamed of my grandmother wrapped in a black shroud laid out on a low table on a stage. I walked through the rooms of a house and found her there though I was looking for Clio. When I saw my grandmother instead I said "swaddle shroud"—

I nursed Clio as my grandmother was lowered into the ground.

Each couplet in the poem requires a full breath and ends when the breath would run out.

—For Clio

—For Helen

(2001)

Collision and Forms of Being in Place: *Linen minus* and *Taken Place*

Linen minus

Linen minus is a collation of necessary and unplanned collisions. Collision in the sense that the book intersects with a time and the conditions of that time—personal conditions and political and historical. It is difficult to think of the book as a container with an outside and inside, since the kind of collision I'm thinking of *can* be marked by an event but also, and moreso, is a continuous state. So as the imprint of a state of continuous collision, the book exceeds its container while, at the same time, the writing between covers and under title, marks a specific collision between surroundings, daily detail, politics, catastrophes, songs, etc., of the book's present; it carries collisions between all of that present and what *seem* to be, and not to be, other times—those re-read and repeated, relived, through reading at the time of this book. The place of the book is a siphon— the lines of vocabulary, political lines…. I was reading a lot of Dorothy Richardson, a lot of theory, editing *HOW(ever)*, living alone, finishing a Ph.D.,… the Amoco oil spill catastrophe in the South of France occurred; Vietnam returned to the popular imagination, this time as a place for tourists to visit; new theories of the creation of the universe were put forward; some people I knew died unthinkable deaths; people I didn't know died in hordes. Richardson spoke of "a growing conviction that the extraneous matter was more essential than the deliberately composed narrative, incidents and figures." (See "Figment of Appointment," above, p. 8)

In this spirit the minus in the title *Linen minus* points to an attempt to empty the work of all but the important extraneous.

Taken Place

If the form of the poem is not sonnet or pantoum or haiku but is motion through place, then the formal constraints of the poem become the forms of being in place.

All but one of the pieces in *Taken Place* have something to do with the kinds of accident that can occur while travelling. The situation of the travel becomes the formal structure: I was presented with or chose the limitations and possibilities lodged in a certain destination at which I arrived, remained for a limited time, with only the books I brought along, the need to eat and sleep, and in most cases, no other familiar person to interfere with or alter the elements of this structure.

I had gone, for example, to the Yucatan—first alone and later accompanied. Mayan pyramids, nativity scenes and other tourists were present as I read the *Popul Vuh*, Heidegger's "Anaximander Fragment," and a collection of the Pre-Socratics. As in a chemical reaction, the books and the place began reading and commenting on each other. All of them, I noticed, were origin stories.

Accident follows *access* in the *O.E.D.*

An accident is an unusual effect of a known cause... an irregular feature in a landscape.

Place as a situation of language, the frame of possible collisions

For Frances Jaffer

Crossing "a great river across the world." —Frances Jaffer[1]

I open Jaffer's book *Alternate Endings* and find papers folded in the back. Two poems sent to me from Frances. Did these poems arrive in the mail yesterday or thirteen years ago?

Crossing a great river. Unable to cross.

Frances and I worked together for many years on *HOW(ever)*, a journal of experimental writing by women working in a modernist tradition and of criticism about contemporary and modernist women's writing. I was very young when I began editing *HOW(ever)* with Frances, Kathleen Fraser, and, at first, Beverly Dahlen. I was in graduate school, but my real education was occurring through my work with *HOW(ever)*. We were all deeply dedicated to the necessity of this project. But my dedication came from a shorter duration of desperation and horror at the treatment of women's writing than theirs. In spite of that they extended an astonishing generosity to me.

Kathleen regularly left the country for almost half the year and Frances and I were then in charge. On an almost daily basis, Frances asked what I thought of a vast range of poetry we were considering for publication. I was shocked that my opinion was of interest. But she kept asking, and her questions required that I articulate what I thought and why. And she did the same. She was not contentious, but she was also not nice, not primarily agreeable. Our friendship was based in curiosity, respect and mutual work. This was the first time I had a friendship with a woman in which we often disagreed and thrived on disagreement. But Frances was not out hunting for a fight. Unlike most people she truly wanted to know what others thought so that she could reconsider what she thought. She pursued doggedly, vehemently—never harshly, sometimes tenderly. We sharpened on each other. I was extremely fortunate to be the recipient of this kind of support and vital conversation when I was so voracious for it and so young.

As was our conversation, Frances's poetry is thought caught in the act of dogged pursuit. It is also full of unmediated brutal declaration and, at the same time, nuanced suggestion of the unsayable. All of her work for at least the last twenty-five years of her life, occurred through a perpetual curtain of illness and pain. The pain kept her on edge. She was burning—living a more lit-up day than some who rarely experience pain or a repeat death threat:

> Dying is good-bye. The absence
>> of me.
>> Unthinkable.
>> Immeasurable. My absence is
>> Absence. It will not be all right.

> —Frances Jaffer, "Dictation"[2]

When Mark Linenthal, Frances' husband, called to tell me Frances had died I said, "The world is a much quieter place now and not for the better."

He said, "I've decided life is part of death, not the other way around, death part of life."

> Inland Passage from a craggy muse a great
> river across the world[3]

How to cross.

(March 1999)

there there: sensation and interruption

—Margaret Tedesco, performance/installation; Oleg Soulimenko, performance; Susan Gevirtz, poetry text; Andrew Klobucar and Susan Gevirtz, soundscape. The LAB, San Francisco. (2000)

Walking into the gallery on to the shore of the show which was not a performance but a place, a convergence of elements that made an environment. Maybe an estuary in late afternoon, more likely the beach of an ocean under the light of sun going down. But not sunset which I think of as an elongated period of time extending into space—more like a suspended expanse of five minutes that went on for three hours and expanded space into its fifth dimensions. This must be what Stein's "continuous present" looks like in the year 2000. This is the "no there" of her "There is no there there." The "no there": a liminal place of tidal repetition without water: huge industrial fan blades relentlessly turning, the face behind the fan splintered and reunited by the blade's motion, the repeated combing, fretting of not getting it straight, the parting of hair, and the comb—implement and sign of gender order, order never done, always done and simultaneously undone by forces bigger, such as wind, or the presence of the girl character, being undone as girl by an infinitesimal and dramatic shift in stance, or the ceasing of fretting as she stood to face the wind head-on and stopped combing arms calmly at her side. This statue this Athena, shape-changer, full flesh embodiment of the sound and sense of the words which were the air in the room was faraway at horizon's edge, then up close; this vulnerable small girl then unmovable monolith, still figure in repetition trance (called our lives?) behind the fan, the shield, the frame of fan, of room, of sound, all in quiet motion, and set again in motion by the occasional impulse, roll of dice, of a dancer whose casual pedestrian steps and poses taken were like visible cut-outs of invisible shapes formed in the atmosphere—if a human could be the shape of weather, or if human form could manifest the weather of human mood as it came into the vast stripped-down sky of the room. The sound, the poetry, was too big to mention—how do you describe words turned to helium putting pressure on the walls as a too small container for their volume? Do you mention air when you describe planes in an air show? How do you recall poetry made into rhythm, urgency, eradication of word through the use of words—medium attenuated and made to be beside itself. We were then beside ourselves, who were for that time not only ourselves. Mirror, echo and first chord, the words which were also only voice, voices, could not be traced to their origin and were not a sole origin—a secret slip of absolute concordance, the soundscape artist on the 7th day making geographies with poetry, as in a "natural" landscape, was in play—all elements, including the lit-up sound board, the mechanisms of the making all present as part of the making, cooperated and at times became the magic carpet by which one arrived inside any land, or conversation conjured by the voice—muted, compressed or almost tripping itself: "the system of script too dry for the ink / within the sore throat / of a system of control"—for example. In oddly spontaneous ritual alignment with the absolute envelopment of word music and of all other elements in the stark, even meditative space, visitors entered quietly and sat along the walls, only occasionally whispering to one another. We could watch each other, witness one another, sink while alone and accompanied into the "impossible light / moat of surround sound."

Delphic Filmic

—for Margaret Tedesco, in response to *Cameo*, her solo performance/
installation in Bay Area Now 4, at Yerba Buena Center for the Arts,
San Francisco (2005)

At first it looked like the film was emanating from her body. As if her body had become a
projector of light and sound. We who entered the small theatre of this performance could
not see the film we could only see her seeing the film and speaking to it. Or of it. Or from
it. The speech—which seemed both hers and not to belong to anyone—had the same
rhythm as the film. The voice, hers, commented on and narrated the events of the film—
not frame by frame, although it felt that way— but scene by scene. *Event* in this narration
included everything from why she, the actress on screen, did that to him, to the report
that he, the actor on screen, looked that way at her, and why. *Event* included what dress
she, the actress, had on, wonder about why a shot of a forest was interspersed in the love
scene, and speculations or propositions about the directors and characters motivations.
Tedesco, the *she* acting, enacting, the film "outside" or to the side of the film, was the
soundtrack, as she'd deleted the sound that originally accompanied the film.

But, while all of that is true, it does not describe the true event of Tedesco's performance.
The true event was the trance that Tedesco entered and in which she remained. The
trance of watching and responding without pause, hesitation, without breaking the rhythm
of the telling of the film or her body, which remained at profile to those of us seated on
the benches in front of her. From here we watched her watching—no, not watching—
inhabiting the film which we couldn't see. Or we stood at another angle and both saw
the film she was seeing and her back—alive, vital, but composed in a poised stillness:
entranced, rarely moving but not "still as a statue" either. Literally a black clothed
"figure" of viewing in a platinum wig.

While her narration sounded spontaneous, just as a film soundtrack does, it must have actually required great preparations. There was an intimacy with the film evident in her speech, a kind of intimacy that can only happen over time. She must have come to know each film she viewed so well that, as with an old friend, she knew something of what to expect, but as with any live being, only to a limited extent. A film may run in the same sequence each time it is viewed but it can never be viewed in exactly the same way. While there was an intimate familiarity there was an equal element of surprise, of not knowing what was coming next, evident in Tedesco's performance. It was precipitous: she did not know what was going to come out of her mouth any more than we did. There was anticipation. What we witnessed made questions, and what we witnessed was question: Was she acting on the film by narrating it and responding to it? Or was the film acting on her, causing her, even demanding that she respond? Was the film the source of her trance or was she encircling, capturing the film with her watch? In all cases we, the viewers of her viewing, were implicated.

The platinum wig was another projecting surface. It repelled any identification with the *her* in front of us as a friend or person with a proper name we could recall. She also did not supply the titles of any of the films she screened. We could wonder about her identity and the name of the film as we sat there almost recognizing, or even knowing, actors, scenes or camera angles. As a bright surface that could have been lifted out of a '40s movie the platinum wig also again signaled Tedesco's position as half in, or half out of the screen— both performer and viewer, and performer of viewer. As a bright surface that emanated light and as "feminine" hair, the wig also made the "her" in front of us a gendered viewer. But not necessarily strictly a woman viewer—any of us can put on and take off a wig.

The performance was relentless. It went on and on without melodrama. It went on for as long as the film—on some evenings that was two hours without pause. The intensity of unfaltering duration was a sight in itself. But not only a sight. We, the viewers of the VIEWER were at least triply mesmerized—by the film, by her presence as an acting/active viewer and narrator of the film, and, as usual, by the camera itself. But who/what was "the camera itself?"

What she said both did and didn't matter. In playing herself as the instrument of this tripled condition, the rhythm of her saying was more important than the what. But speech always begs the question of address—was this narration for those of us who wandered into her part of the gallery? Or was it like weather, a phenomenon to which we are all subject and through her performance got to witness from afar? Was it like a storm front moving across a plate glass window?—A phenomenon to witness, to overhear or to eavesdrop on? Or was the narration a way to caress the film? A way to speak with and to it, them, our real lovers, in case we hadn't noticed by now?

In this sense Tedesco, in her bright cave at Yerba Buena, was uttering an urtext of our social moment—speaking aloud that which we never hear (except distractedly in our own minds for a second) and in that sense perhaps there was something prophetic in her voicing. Cassandra goes to the cinema and reminds us aloud of what's to come, through her acute seeing of, reporting on, how we now see?

For a long time I sat and watched. Or sat and listened, not sure of which was the primary perception—utterly entranced by her trance and the play of sound, light and motion—of attribution and quotation—as it washed over us.

The films screened in Tedesco's performance *Cameo* included Orson Wells' *The Trial*, Atom Egoyan's *The Adjuster*, Francis Ford Coppola's *The Conversation*, and Robert Wise's *The Haunting*, among others.

Paros Symposium Opening

The Paros Symposium is an annual meeting of Greek and U.S. poets, translators, and editors. The symposium, which met for the first time in 2004, was motivated in the words of its organizers, Greek poet Siarita Kouka and U.S. poet Susan Gevirtz, in the hope of "altering our orientations to our own languages and writing, as well as expanding our understanding of the social contexts in which we (respectively) make our work. Observing that we were not alone in this hope and these needs, we proceeded to invite others." The symposium met for six years during the last week of June on the island of Paros, and for five of those years at "The House of Literature." In the seventh year the symposium met at the European Cultural Center of Delphi. The "House of Literature" was so named by EKEMEL, the European Center for the Translation of Literature and the Human Sciences, responsible also for recently renovating an old hotel and transforming it into an international meeting place for translators, poets, editors, journalists, and many other kinds of writers. EKEMEL is subsidized by EKEBI, the National Book Center of Greece. It has been our honor to be invited to hold the symposium at EKEMEL and EKEBI's House of Literature.

The following is the opening address to the group gathered to begin the June 2006 Paros Symposium. The group included Greek and Anglophone poets participating in the symposium, the then new director of EKEMEL and Catalan translator Natividad Galvez Garcia, and Greek poet Ioanna Abramivou, translator of Paul Celan and Walter Benjamin, among other poets and translators in residence at The House of Literature on Paros.

Welcome. We begin, as we did last year, at the fortuitous time of the summer solstice and the feast of St John the Diviner. Many divinatory customs are practiced in Greece on this occasion. Greek poet George Seferis reminds us of one example: the dropping of molten lead into "speechless water." This is water that a child has carried secretly from a well, without speaking to or answering anyone met along the way. The future is foretold from the shape the lead assumes when it hardens in the water. This story of translation from fluid metal into the silence of water, into the fluidity of words about the future, or into some as yet unspoken futures of words, accompanies us in our seven days together. It is also emblematic of the purpose of our meeting. We approach the idea of translation as a multitude of possible alchemies: the literal word-for-word work of moving between languages; the conversations that are generated in talking about and thinking of approaches to the work; methodic or other inventions that become necessary in response to the difficulties and impossibilities built into our tasks—to mention only a few.

Each year there are some participants who wish for specific and uniform guidelines regarding the methods of approach to translation that we prefer. And there are others who feel constrained by any mention of method. Now that we have the momentum of a few years, translation and contact between participating poets occurs not only during, but also before and after our in-person meetings. For example, the Greek American poet John Sakkis, who was here last year, translated a book by Greek poet Siarita Kouka in time for last year's symposium; Demosthenes Agrafiotis has had work translated and published in an American magazine this year; the editors of other American magazines are asking us for work by Greek poets in Greek and in English; EKEBI, The National Book Center of Greece has expressed interest in publishing work by all of the poets involved in this year's symposium; this is to mention only a few examples of the kinds of exchange in the realm of publication that has resulted from our meetings.

Greek poetry is also getting airplay in the States through the live medium of poetry readings: Steve Dickison, director of the Poetry Center and American Poetry Archives at San Francisco State University, invited Siarita Kouka and her translator John Sakkis to read in May of 2005. After the reading there was a discussion about translation and contemporary Greek poetry. The audience, composed mainly of students, American and Greek-American poets, participated in a lively question and answer period. I recently opened a poetry reading by reading the English translations of the poet George Koukaledes' work made when he was here last year—and the Greek American poet Eleni Stecoupolos read the work in Greek. In this vein, we also hope to understand more about the public and private lives of poetry in our respective countries. In contrast to last year, the American poets here this year are all from San Francisco and from a loose but somehow specific and coherent community of poets that is very internationally oriented. In San Francisco there are more poetry reading series, poet's theatre and performance events, than it is possible to attend. Many are involved in translation, some poets open their homes to make a place for what are called "house readings," or to honor a newly published book with a party and reading. Steve Dickison is responsible for inviting poets from all over the world to read at The Poetry Center, and there is a sense of collaboration among many San Francisco writers—sometimes at the level of the work itself, and often in service of creating this public life. I think that I can safely speak in the plural and say that we who are here from San Francisco share a need for exposure to the poetry and poets of other places.

There are many different relations to Greek and English present in this room, from native speakers, to Greek Americans, to Greeks fluent in English to varying degrees, to Americans knowing little or no Greek but steeped in poetry, therefore acute listeners and dedicated to curiosity. The asymmetry in the room is also impossible to ignore: all of the Greeks in the room know some English and few of the Americans know much Greek. Needless to say this is symptomatic of a larger global situation. So as Americans we have gratitude to the Greeks not only for hosting us in a literal, but also in a figurative house of language.

We begin here, as everywhere, with the fact that we often cannot understand one another—and of course I don't speak here only of Greeks and Americans. This makes listening to that which we don't understand, whether it be in our "own" language, or in a second, or an unknown language, perhaps the first essential and enduring act of writing and translation. Thus, while production is important it is not our main concern—we are more interested in the unexpected conversations on and off paper that result from our time together—and that will continue beyond this time in surprising ways. So when we convene tomorrow morning we will divide into groups of two or three or more and choose a poem, or a page from a poem, to dwell on for some hours or days—unsure of the outcome.

If all that occurs in our time here is a more acute listening, an exposure to that which otherwise would not have been heard, even a flicker of recognition of the impossible to hear—it will have been a very generative stay together.[1]

(2006)

Letter: Translation Panel Invitation

Dear Judith, David, and Brandon—

Thanks for the invitation to participate on this panel. I've been thinking about it and I have to respond in this way:

First, I am really not a translator. This is a somewhat different "not" from the "not" in Norma Cole's wonderful and useful piece "Why I Am Not A Translator."

I am a riveted up-close voyeur of translation. I am committed to it in some sort of inescapable way—I am captured by it, captive to it. I am a translator wannabe. Many mornings every week I go first to my infant Greek books and sit with my dictionary writing out words, letter by letter, taking great kinesthetic pleasure in what might be happening—a cypher and a kind of sense—and a hope of learning something. But I really do not know enough Greek to do anything that could approximate the full complexity that involves being able to swim and breathe in another language like Norma or Stacy Doris or Chet Wiener or Brandon Brown or so many others we know (and so many we don't know), that could be called translation.

That said, I am also always in a state of translating as writing. So for me to pick out translation from one language to another as the only kind of writing that = translation is to obfuscate the myriad acts of translation that go on in language and in the work of some writers all the time. After a conversation we recently had about this, Larry Kearney wrote a wonderful series of poems called "Translations" in which he translated poems originally in English by Stevens, Auden, and many others, into poems written in other Englishes. In this kind of translating there is no possibility of anything like one-to-one correspondences between exact words.

Not that there is between, i.e., English and Greek, or French and English, either.

I am further not a translator because, as I said above, I know little Greek, having studied for only 3 years, and because I am first a mute, though it may not sound that way, and I am chock-full of weird dyslexias, alexias, asphyxias, counterlexias, and memory processing quirks, that come to bear in all language. It's hard to *say* much in or about Greek yet. And this is really a different state from a person who does not consider herself a translator but is fluent in and beyond her first language. I'm really not sure I'm even fluent in my first language.

There is also being translated by place. And translation by exposure: one immerses oneself in a situation—for example, in a cauldron surrounded by the sounds of Greek, the weather, the ways of eating, sleeping, driving, drinking,... in that place—and one's mode of explaining the world to oneself is altered and mixed up. Translation of one's senses, of one's sense of sequence like a grammar of proceeding in the 3-D, is impacted by vicinity and contagion.

Not to mystify, but to acknowledge that being out of place [ec-static], in an utterly new place where even the road signs are startling, can have a great impact, can destabilize one's first language as well as one's ways of proceeding that are part of the first language/social milieu including appetites, bodily energies, health....

In addition to this physicality of being translated by place in Greece (though it could happen anywhere), for me there is also having one's poetry translated into Greek while sitting next to and working closely with a Greek poet-translator. A very profound embodiment—maybe like being next to the musician instead of having the CD on in the room. Or maybe improvisation itself. For hours and hours we discuss and grapple with the fabulous illuminating minutiae of words inside of words, of contended histories inside of and associated with particular words, of the sounds and their maybe impossible to explain music and sense, of the politics of how and who gets to or got to speak when and where, and of course much more.

All of this profoundly alters one's relation to and hearing of one's own work and one's "own" language. Among other things, one gets literally and figuratively read back to oneself.

While I can barely translate, there are few necessities or pleasures bigger than being in the midst of it. This is the really selfish and shameless truth about why, with Greek poet Siarita Kouka, I started the Paros Translation and Conversation Symposium that has been meeting now for four years. Whether I can "do" it or not, or to what extent, it is evident to me that translation is inescapable, that it's the only responsible—and I mean that in the fullest sense of *ability to respond*—act for Americans and others, but especially for Americans in the current political climate. Insisting on this has a different inflection for one holding an American passport than for anyone else. As Siarita recently said (in English), "Believe me, if you weren't American they wouldn't be so quick to invite us back every year— If you were Czech or Bosnian or something else this symposium wouldn't get so much attention from the Greek authorities."

Again, thank you for asking me to participate on this panel. If you would like me to talk about these kinds of things I would be glad and honored to do that. But I would also be happy and honored to be in the audience if you decide instead to invite someone who is a translator. You really may want to do that. It really may be much more appropriate and of interest to have someone like Eleni Stecopoulos, who was the Symposium guest organizer for Anglophone poets this year, or any number of other translators to be on this interesting panel and usher Brandon's play into the 3-D world.

All best,
Susan

(2007)

71

A Brief Picture Book for Barbara Guest

When Barbara Guest first moved to Berkeley about twelve years ago she had a second floor studio in Albany in what had once been a girl's school. That is when our tradition of picnics began. Besides Dorothy Richardson, we both had great fascination with Los Angeles, dolmas, kasseri cheese, black cured olives, hotels, Robert Walser, *Close Up*, movies, H.D. of course....

I would knock on the half open door of the studio. Once when I came in she pointed to the blackboard. On it were words written long ago in chalk that became a poem from that time. *Quill, Solitary* APPARITION was published in 1996, perhaps the poem from the chalkboard is in that book. Maybe:

> WHISPER, or

> *perhaps a mere tale (the hair combing) placed*
> *on a smooth surface*

> contrasts with her

> griefless OWLERY

> *'throughout time and its dungeon'*...

> —Barbara Guest, from the poem
> "Quill, Solitary *Apparition*"[1]

We had our picnics in the big scrubby field in front of the school. By noon, as the fog burned off, it smelled of wild anise heating up. From the table we ate on we could see a bit of the bay—our "view."

When she gave up the studio the picnics moved inside. Along with food, I sometimes brought flowers to stand in for the field. After one picnic Barbara sent me some photos of the house after I left, a postcard of "me" she had recently found, and a note which said:

> Susan,
>
> I breakfasted on food of the gods this morning, having supped their nectar, thanks to you. You should have witnessed our photographing the flowers, they were magnificent this morning, and cheered me into daily living.
>
> You're tossing your head as you go out the door.
>
> Ever, ever, ever thine
>
> B.

The message is dated 29 March 2002. It is now, 30 March 2006. The loss of Barbara is really too big to address yet, but she had anticipated this and so much else. So I rely on her for the words, again from that early picnic era:

> Palm tree
> as subject—moonlight arranges
> and branch, within the courtyard
>   a bronze capitalization
> dares to remember—.

>   gift of oneself to this order;
>   for the sake of virtuosity, its primrose
>   need of defining.

(2006)

Interior photos by Barbara Guest. Flowers brought by Susan Gevirtz
to Barbara Guest's home at 1301 Milvia Street, Berkeley, California in
2002. Two views of the sitting room with pink Joe Stefanelli painting.

Postcard given to Susan Gevirtz with photographs. Image: Head of
Dionysos, with wreath of vine leaves, 1st century A.D., from Museum
of Corinth, Greece.

Orders

Anyone watching the sky with the naked eye from Earth will notice that, apart from the steadily moving Sun and Moon, there are five *wandering* stars: the five planets of antiquity. These, and the newly discovered planets, appear to move around the Earth roughly following the Sun's annual circle, the *elliptic* or *zodiac*. If only life was this simple! Watch planets for any length of time, and, far from moving in any simple way, they lurch around like drunken bees, waltzing and whirling. Occasionally, when planets pass, or kiss, each appears to the other to *retrogress*, or go backward, against the stars for a time. This was once common knowledge.

—John Martineau*

First order—wonder—

Preliminary orders—Tending of the parent before s/he's a parent invokes the child before it's flesh

　　"What would your life be like now without me?"
she says at 9 yrs old

The ability to frame the question is imagination / condition

The necessity: kindle bonfires and keep throwing things in

The baby gives the orders around here and it's called "listening"

Over there it's called spoilage and somewhere else it's called

taxonomy

the child is a collection of terms:

Conscription Grotto　　　　　　　Circumspection

meta   'odos   Ode of the method of wild fire

the anti place   when you get possessed

"less than useless"   you become 4 letters   Hunger   Ardor   Water

you can't count higher than the song of the open road
you can't replace b o o k with b a b y   production as reproduction
CONFLAGRATION   When you get possessed you are both   It finds you out that
refrain

condition
decoration
sequence [rhythm
serial command
diatribe
ordinal
tactic
ordinance
ordination
coordination
chronological alphabetical Call to order Under orders So stricken by the ordinary
extraordinary

each appears to the other to go backward
against common knowledge
coincident
you you and you showed up in "my" life

clearly no longer mine
as if it ever was

Ungraven

middle voice verb
what you get done for yourself
is not a checklist
something more like a damned position of privilege: exile, debasement, to be the
Apostrophe, the one, the source, of loathing, the one from which one turns away in
aversion abhorrence, the one one comes from, unavoidable our denotation, separation, the
contrary and it's Restoration

venturing into the underbrush atmosphere
fear and fear alike   Axis of access
in excess of verb and explanation   Who is susceptible to explanation?

                              If sound = touch at a distance

Bossed around

"please"

◇◇◇◇◇◇◇

THIRD APPREHENSION

Doctor Editor

> Though one may say that I have told nothing new, the arrangement of the material is my own.
>
> —Pascal

Shaking Hands

Once the poem is sent, it becomes the patient under the eye of the Doctor Editor.

> The illness "discovered" through the interview is constructed, not found. A diagnosis is a way of interpreting and organizing observations. It is no less real because it is critically dependent on what physicians ask and what they hear, and on what patients report and do not report than it would be if it were based on the results of physical examinations and laboratory tests. Since the discovered illness is, in this sense, partly a function of the talk between a patient and a physician, the study of this talk is central to our understanding.[1]

Every poem is potentially ill. The poem arrives, and the Doctor meets it in her or his office. The meeting is usually without witness, without audience. The Doctor must learn from the patient why she or he has come. This is not a sociable relationship and yet it has a protocol:

> 1. When meeting a new patient in your office, would you shake hands with him?

> Answer: Social handshaking occurs primarily when two men meet initially or when they have been apart for some time. Shaking hands is much less frequent among women. As a social custom, shaking hands is not as prevalent in the United States as it was 50 years ago, or as it now is in Europe. Shaking hands in a physician's office is not common. After all, it is not a sociable relationship. From another outlook, some valuable information can be obtained from the handshake (whether the hand is limp or firm, wet or dry, steady or shaking, clumsy or agile, deformed or normal). The only rule is to shake hands if it is the comfortable thing to do for you and the patient.[2]

The second the physician lays hands on the poem, diagnosis begins. Is the poem deformed or normal, in need or replete, shaky, sweaty, and where does it fall in a range between illness and health? These are the kinds of questions that the poem may elicit from the Doctor Editor. In the initial moments of the interview, even the author's name may shape the nature of contact. It may suggest the bodily contours or color of an imagined author and determine which social customs follow. As a consequence, it may or may not be comfortable to shake hands.

Since the discovered illness is partly a function of the talk between the editor and the writing, the extent to which the Doctor Editor engages in *a study of this talk is central to our understanding.* Whether or not the Doctor Editor takes a double watch, attending to her or his own method of organizing observations (and thus constructing the writing in hand) and at the same time listening closely to the report of the poem, will have significant impact.

Patient Utterances

> The fact that psychic processes may lead to somatic symptoms… lays upon the physician a special responsibility in regard to his behavior toward the patient…. First of all he must remember that his every utterance and act, as well as every therapeutic measure, has a suggestive effect on the patient, only too often of a harmful nature.[3]

Illness or health is "discovered" through a conversation that may occur between the poem and the editor—but, what is the patient? The writer or the poem or the talk between the poem and the editor? And who is the editor? The one who is perpetually in a state of diagnosis, or the one who has gnosis? The kinds of questions asked will also determine what counts as a poem, the condition discovered in it—even whether illness and health are at issue.

1. Several examples of questions that will yield "no" answers of unknown meaning are as follows:[4]

A.   Have you been sick before?

B. Do you kick your dog?
C. Do you smoke excessively?

2. Rewrite the following questions so that they do not suggest the answers.

A. Has the pain gone into your left arm from your chest?
B. May I assume you have taken the medicine as directed?
C. Before taking the medicine do you always try to relieve the pain by resting?

Does the act of interpretation also become an object of investigation for the Doctor Editor—or is the Doctor Editor in an ice cream parlor choosing his or her favorite flavor? Taste is made from favorite flavors:

> Like chocolate   even vanilla
> chocolate   strawberry   sasparilla
> Flavors are electric
> try to get a shocker
>
> —Public Enemy[5]

Are favorite flavors learned or genetically inherited?

What profile, mugshot, bust, portrait, composite, does taste take on the page?

Adjuvant Data

The patient's narrative may be assisted, prevented or perverted. Other options may exist if adjuvant data are sought or imagined:

> Adjuvant data are supporting information available to the physician about his patient. Examples are the patient's posture, behavior, style of dress, voice quality, and modulation and the physician's own reactions to the patient.[6]

The patient is not a neutral zone.

Now it sometimes happens that a belief… transforms itself into a memory.[7] And then, "taking" a case becomes an act of remembering the patient's past for the patient. Who is hungry for the past? The Doctor may mistake the traditions of the past for her or his present opinion. The Editor who does not seek adjuvant data is at the mercy of her or his beliefs.

The Ward and the Word

> The perspective of a person in the scientific attitude is that of a "disinterested" observer. Events in the world are not viewed within subjective coordinates of space and time, but with reference to abstract, standard, and context-free coordinates of "objective" space and time. Events and actions receive their meaning from their location in a general scheme or model from which pragmatic motives have been removed. Interest in the world is theoretical.[8]

The recent history of the Doctor and that of the Editor collide in psychoanalysis. Psychoanalysis—the method of interpretation that discovers "the woman question." And Freud, the Editor Writer of the conversation between the Doctor and the Patient. The "woman question" is one question among many possible other questions, that can provide a historical location for thinking about the diagnostic nature of the editorial act. Since events and actions receive their meaning from their location, pragmatic motives can only be traced through material context. Interest in the world can then be more and less than theoretical.

If the profile of the writing is difficult to decipher, too 'easy,' or eludes diagnosis entirely, the Doctor Editor might decide to do further research on the historical conditions out of which the writing arises. In this hypothetical case Dr. Editor will begin research on the historical locations of his or her own modern origins and the coinciding cultural conditions in which early twentieth-century British and American women writers found themselves. These writers inherited the predominantly white and middle class debate around "the woman question."

With a large increase of women writing in the nineteenth-century one of the main issues around which the "woman question" debates revolved was women's proper relation to writing and literature. These discussions, rampant in medical journals, psychoanalytic discourse, the popular press, and elsewhere, focused on the links between sexuality and art:

> In [mid-nineteenth-century] discussions of women and literature, the sexually laden language suggests two theories. According to one, female imagination is a volatile and highly erotic force that must be repressed, or at least controlled; according to the other, women's writing is a sign of sexual and emotional frustration. Both must be seen against the prevailing assumption that artistic creation is, like the sexual act, a male activity in which women have only an extremely restricted part. As the *Saturday Review* reminds readers in 1865, "Female nature, mental as well as physical, is essentially receptive and not creative."[9]

From the mid-to-late Victorian period there was a remarkable increase of madness, of institutionalization, and of publication among women. At that time, and on into the early twentieth-century, the contradictory demands and expectations on women to be, in the midst of an increasingly industrialized society, representatives of "feminine" purity and order, and to be perfectly controlled in their conduct and skilled in domestic managerial capacities, coincided with a growing fear of female sexuality.[10]

Freud's main investigation of issues related to the "woman question" centered on his studies of hysterics, almost all female.[11] As a result of his research, one of Freud's many observations was that, "The mechanism of poetry is the same as that of hysterical phantasies."[12] Freud is useful to this discussion not only as one of the most famous Doctor Editors of this century, but also because his work voiced many of the obsessions and anxieties prevalent in the late-Victorian, early-modernist moment.

And so, the conditions and consequences of many of Freud's formulations can be seen as symptomatic of widespread cultural views. For example, in the above formulation all poetry is potentially coded "hysterical" and "feminine." In the larger culture this code presented an at least double problem for women writers who already dangerously occupied the realm of the monstrous in their display of inappropriate excess, manifest in the desire to write, and their excited imaginations evident in the writing itself. According to the "woman question" debates, it was implied, and sometimes prescribed, that women who wrote or did anything "creative" must be controlled by husbands, doctors or institutions. A writing woman, or a woman who was active in any realm outside the domestic, contradicted her "nature" by being a "creative" agent rather than a passive and receptive container.

While it is true that poetry, like the hysteric, was symbolically coded feminine in the dominant cultural discourse of late-Victorian, early-modern Europe and the United States, some hysterics were actually male, though symptoms of hysteria were often differently diagnosed when observed in male patients, and many poets were, of course, men. The gendering of poetry as feminine in the dominant cultural discourse required of many male poets a defensive stance: some felt the need to demonstrate that they were emphatically not feminine, not mentally or physically ill, that while a man's poetry might partake of the mechanism of hysterical phantasies, he did not.[13]

This foray into a turn-of-the-century context and history, however radically truncated, hopefully suggests what might be at stake, and what might be missed or overlooked, in the diagnostic editorial conversation if adjuvant data is not sought. Since diagnostic judgments occur in and are artifacts of the network of cultural discourses that exist at the historical moment in which the editor or doctor lives, and the tradition in which she or he was trained, diagnoses are never neutral—but are always results of inherited and inhabited assumptions. Although taste may not change as a result of the editor's further research, diagnosis may at least become a more complicated act.

Types of Errors

It would be an error to think that the woman question debates have ended.
It would be an error to think we are not all inheritors.

> As medical students we make many errors in evaluating patients…. One kind of mistake arises from your own lack of knowledge of what is known, or culpable ignorance.[14]

It would be an error to think you have finished imagining your own history.

In *The Discourse of Medicine*, Mishler says that one of the main elements and dangers of the medical interview is the "process of selective attention on the physician's part." He goes on to say,

> He [the physician] responds to one element of the patient's account, usually her mention of a specific symptom, abstracts it from the context in which it is presented, and then refers to the symptom within another context expressed in the voice of medicine. The symptom is thus transformed by being relocated to a different province of meaning…. much is lost in the translation from one voice to another. It is as if a poem in one language that uses qualities of the weather, such as its dampness or coldness, as a metaphor for the feeling state of the narrator were to be translated literally into another language as a description of the weather.[15]

Selective attention is a universal phenomenon. And if you have ever tried to pack for the tropics while snow falls outside your window, you know that the editor's weather condition usually becomes the only season and place of reference. All other narrative positions and climatic zones are theoretical.

Face to Mask Interaction

> Although two persons are talking to each other in the medical interview, it does not have the essential reciprocity feature of ordinary face-to-face interaction and might more precisely be viewed as face-to-mask interaction.[16]

When I was a Doctor Editor on *HOW(ever)*, I found out repeatedly how present the turn-of-the-century (marked 1900) is in the late twentieth-century. Without access to that history, gestured at above, I would not have known that many reactions to *HOW(ever)* were still riddled with the tones and obsessions of the woman question debates. One of the most overt examples was evident in a copy of a review of the May 1984 issue of *HOW(ever)* by Robert Peters, sent to us by a male poet friend.[17] In the last paragraph of his review Peters says,

I have yet to meet anyone who has been able to sit and read Gertrude Stein for more than one hour at a stretch (Kenneth Rexroth alone has had the balls to say so in print), or to remain excited by H.D. after twenty pages or so. These seem the primary goddesses behind this sort of writing. A poem is not a dictionary. A poem is not a set of easy metaphysical speculations on the nature of grammar, guilt or the primal flood….. Let's not keep the trope flying, let's strangle the little creature in his crib before he soils his pants and screws up our life.[18]

There's not that much new to say about the infant poem invoked in the above paragraph. Could there be a more alive-and-well embodiment of high anxiety about women's relation to writing than the baby in a cradle at the center of this crèche scene? The infant poem (above) is a pre-socialized (not yet toilet-trained), necessarily male "creature"—not yet fully human. The poem is male since, in this framework, it would be impossible to imagine a legit poem as anything but an adored son—even if the mechanism by which he enters the world is hysterical phantasy via an unnatural and dangerous goddess. This infant—a result of excess, and himself excessive (like a dictionary) and boring (after twenty pages or so) might, if not strangled first, return as tropes or viruses return, to spread excrement all over the white sheets of the page and "screw up our life."

Their Life, still composed of a Victorian cleanliness and order, the life that the Doctor Editor-Poet in the above paragraph shares with some of his medical colleagues, is a life free of the ambiguity of diagnosis. Its flavor is vanilla, its crime is easy metaphysical speculation about grammar. Balls in print are its anti-mascot. In this world a poet knows what a poem is and is not, and she who produces "this sort of writing," should beware of strangulation.

(February 1994)

◊◊◊◊◊◊

I was an associate editor on *HOW(ever)* from 1985–1989. I remain in gratitude to Kathleen Fraser and all who participated in the *HOW(ever)* project as writers and editors. And to the legacy of that community, in which I, and so many women writers, now live.

Postscript

Looking back at this from the vantage of 2011, there's not much I want to add or change—just to say that in the span of time between the writing of this in 1994 and the present I have witnessed many more 'face to mask' interactions and still do not think Robert Peter's words mark an exception, a special case, or a kind of diagnosis that we as a culture are over and done with.

(2011)

A Place Ajar

> We needed a place on the model of heaven and hell, not quite one, not quite the other, but both at the same time. A place ajar, for closure is intolerable, unacceptable to the mind.
>
> —Edmond Jabès

> I am the narrator in whose accident I speak
>
> —*Domino: point of entry**

At the end of *Planet of the Apes,* Charlton Heston rides bareback with the beautiful mute human female straddling the horse behind him. They gallop along the beach where a large unidentifiable form emerges in the distance. Heston's face contorts into sudden horror and comprehension as they get close enough to see. It is the upper torso of the big mother-man, the statue of liberty, lying half unburied on the shore, waves lapping over her sand-submerged lower half. This sight triggers the revelation that he and his fellow space explorers have not crashed on an alien planet in the opening of the movie but back on earth in the future. The world as they know it has long ago vanished.

Does this vision register the collective fantasy of a return, or first trip to the mother's body capsized in the inner seams of outer space? We have existed under the mandatory canopy of abandoning the corporeal for the air above. Our astronauts hatched from Zeus' head? Born from the space-womb?

Often a past that never happened serves to register the conditions of the present. The past is lodged in the future in so many movies now. In the *Planet of the Apes* version of the end there is a strange nostalgia for the amniotic ocean—we spend a long wordless time watching the couple ride along the beach having escaped into the "forbidden zone" beyond the borders of the ape civilization. Is this a nostalgia for the mother who, like Athena, signals the utopic male-run city state, and stands in front of it, guarding it and welcoming aliens to it? But who are the civilized and who are the barbarians in the ape-run state? Which mother is it—a man in drag as a woman who sentences women to the realm of the hearth? Is the mother's body animal, vegetable or metal? A nostalgia for contact with a past that never existed.

The body is the broken jar between. The lapse that disappears and reappears and gives us away again. And takes us. And brings us back. If the realm of apocalypse is disclosure, the revelation of the future is in the figure lying on shore, metal made flesh.

> You are all still there
> bodies I once knew but now beheaded

> *—Linen minus*

"It's hard to tell the beginning from the end," said a friend while describing the new quick and lethal strep virus that takes inches off your throat in hours, currently striking, mainly in England. Invasive Group A Streptococcus. "Viruses have intention," he said, which made me wonder, which lines locate or decimate something? How invasive is meaning? Where is none? Where does intention meet decimation?

Each time she says
she says, "this is the last"
Sweet immolation fastens desire

> *—Domino*

We can't exactly see the future while it sees us, but we always inhabit it. And can watch it on video.

Lost in appearance the more
I see you the more you are gone

> *—Taken Place*

If we disappear, isn't it only we as we have known us?
Maybe, like memory and amnesia, we go away as we
stay. And actually the bacteria and microbes that are
our fabric go on as us, without us, in spite of, because
of us, in a mutual wet feast.

> close your eyes
> these are
> the last days
> of the
> future

—*Taken Place*

In a world where legal truth and testimony have fully revealed their inadequacy, we rely
now on confessions of the unremembered. It is impossible to write in the face of perpetual
accident—the face on the front page "AGONY IN RAWANDA"—when the accident of
being alive, of being sentenced to life is, even at its best, unbearable.

the fullest speech blinded
speech

> —*Domino*

But how, even with all of our severe luck, can we go on? It is as a gift to
the dead and the not yet alive that we attempt to recall something that hasn't yet
happened.

> Who remember all that has occurred is all
> that was available to occur

> —*Linen minus*

How do we measure the distance of this return? Is it held by the journey between the wreckage of the spacecraft that opens *Planet of the Apes* and the fallen statue in the end? Or is it registered on the face of the one woman astronaut found dead in the spacecraft debris? The face of the one who was slated to continue the human race claimed now by light years of wrinkles.

So we
were sent
and following
followed. Memories
before our time. We
backwards think and
on paper inherit
contour, what to call it?
We our readers' readers
Not knowing where
leaving off begins.

—*Prosthesis* :: *Caesarea*

Interpretation and reinterpretation, which equal writing, are optimistic acts. They assume there is a next time. They invite, hope for, want another. Apocalypse signals the end of interpretation. But when you watch *Road Warrior* you can see how fantastically and fatally optimistic it is to imagine the end. *Road Warrior* begins "after the end of the world." Everyone pursues the "juice" (gasoline) which is driven north in a revived tanker truck. Almost everyone is killed protecting or chasing the tanker, except Mel Gibson, the Feral Kid, and a few bad guys. And then, in the end of the end, Gibson takes the fuel cap off and sand pours out of the big metal hull. Is the future always like that, a decoy that keeps us driving?

in letters immortality
no messianic wait
for words
words

secure the coming world

Who the true follower
Who false?

passionate territory
of message

—*Prosthesis :: Caesarea*

It's always more a question of duration than possibility: Not, do we have a future? or, Are we now in the end? (Because the answer to both of those is always yes.) Instead, "I didn't know how long we'd have together. [But then again] Who does?"

— Harrison Ford, *Blade Runner*

(January 26, 1995)

Uneven Uneventfulness: Kathleen Fraser's *Discrete Categories Forced into Coupling*

—for Kathleen Fraser

If a writer was allowed to fold one critical essay into the pages of one of her books, so that the essay might fall into the lap of a future reader, Fraser might slip Burton Hatlen's "Zukofsky As Translator" into *Discrete Categories Forced into Coupling.*[1]

Recently she handed me a copy of that essay. Next to the word "TRANSLATOR" in the title she had written and underlined the word *Transmutation.*

From the first section of *Discrete Categories* titled "*Champs* (fields) & between"[2]:

3. The air came down like rice. It scattered through unevenness and uneventfulness.

came down   unevenness

The first two sentences of the Hatlen essay read:

> "To Zukofsky," Creeley says, "poetry represents a way of seeing words as in the world in much the same way that men are." Words and men alike are "in the world," to Zukofsky, "as material objects."[3]

The Air

"The air came down like rice."

                  like

"It scattered through unevenness and uneventfulness."

————

The air   The rice   scattered

    The words uneven   the event of

    them   an unevent

that the poem marks.

Fraser's *like* as Hatlen's *alike* ("words and men alike") transmutes air, words, the actions: "came down" and "scattered" into the material *rice* and into the words we can touch and see on the page, and into the material of the human that is not touchable, that is the time of the unevent, and the feeling of unevenness.

The Materials of the Material

In that alchemy time is also shown to be material in nature. While made and presented here, time remains unnamed but palpable, and so does it's passing. The modernist revelation that the subject is no subject—or is the minutia that has not traditionally occupied the subject position (in both senses) is revealed again here and given a contemporary twist. Fraser renders a treatment of banality and description through a kind of hyperrealism in which the material of words, human bodies, rice, air and many other objects turn into one another by the transmutations she performs throughout *Discrete Categories*. Air into rice—by the magic of simile; uneven into unevent—by the addition of one letter that changes one non-thing into another entirely different non-thing; and by a cutting and splicing that creates a sense synesthesia—which changes the intangible coming down of air that cannot be seen, into the imagined coming down of rice, which would be seen and felt, into a coming down of the uneven gaps between the drops of implied falling rain that could be seen.

The Unevent

In *Discrete Categories* the unevent is not a non event.

It is a space-time in which nothing happens except transmutation.

Fraser names this space-time through the objects and subjects of the mundane. Using this kind of hyperrealistic description, that seems to spring from acute observation, reportage and imagining of that which presents itself on any day.

While Fraser uses simile, there is also no simile or metaphor operating here. There is no comparison of like to unlike things, instead there is a perpetual motion of things and states and humans becoming, which is not like an immersion in actual language but is an actual immersion.

Seeing Things

Fraser underlines "But the Zukofskys remind us that the 'littera,' the letter, is an aural and visual shape, not a 'meaning.'"[4]

An inventory of kinds of transmutation that occur throughout *Discrete Categories* reveals a continual return to the visual, a refiguration of the visual, as a kind of imaginal pivot through which, on which, kinds of transmutation turn and return.

A few examples:

—Film stills and out-takes

"a cinematic event"   "…again a swerving laid out to any random viewer, in this case herself a cinematic event to which she would gradually attach herself as she drove forward and slowly shifted gears through the lengthening."[5]

—Photos and the process of being turned into a photo

"Why must the photograph of the two of them come out of its envelope every year and be pinned to the wallpaper?"[6]

"A. still believes D. is the girl he thought she was and continues describing her to herself, even as tree bark is creeping between her thighs and pushing from roots that lift her body higher with the force of minute-by-minute growth."

 "exposing the anatomy of imagined capture…."

—"You can hear her breathing in the photograph"[7]

The process of being turned into a photograph in this poem is also the process of Daphne being chased and turned into a tree, or a member of a family being fixed into one role in that family, or Bernini fixing Daphne and Apollo in a sculpture, or a museum photographer capturing that sculpture in a photo.

—Windows, Drawings of windows

"During the second half of their marriage, her first husband had drawn a window in oil pastels…. She looked at this picture every day, even carrying it to her new house ten years later upon marrying a second man. The window pulled her into an unnamed world: its grainy surface concealing and exposing something unfinished, so that the turquoise curtain, being closer to expected light, became a defined plane beyond which she might retrieve each vagrant thought."

—from "pressure," in "You can hear her breathing in the photograph"[8]

—Paint, painting

> She gives you her colors when you scrape her down and layer her
> again with rose madder bleached by repetitions of white in the width
> of big
>
> embankments, as if you thought of her
>   as a road to somewhere called "dedication to light
>
>   —"notebook 5: in spite of gradual deficits"[9]

—Depiction on tracing paper

> You, yourself may remember a map
>
> in which the colors bear no relation
> to the terrain they represent.
> the ocean growing lighter and lighter
>
> or its depiction (traced on thin paper)
> hangs over it, touching and leaving a smudge.
>
>   —"notebook 2: radiant inklings"[10]

—Geometric memory bank

") —I will mark this space as a kind of geometric memory bank, not so much to contain or trap the sentence but to give it a place to rest, once I find it, or even where it might reconstitute itself outside of the context in which it was first discovered.

The sentence, of course, will be different once it has been retrieved."

—"Soft pages"[11]

Letterbox screen, mail slot, soft bed of the soft page on which words can rest, savings account for memory, new context for the soon to arrive new sentence, container, frame, marker of the future difference of the sentence once it has been retrieved and altered by its loss, window, hole through which to spy on the mysterious geometry of memory

"To show the images between the images"

—Chantal Ackerman[12]

No orgasm, murder, birth, starvation, war
Instead
indifference
Fraser as purveyor of indifference, but indifference as a kind of care. Tending with relentless scrutiny to that which often receives indifference
weather, traffic, cooking,
scrutiny of the different kinds of indifference manifest in bodies, as flesh, language, the monument, the moment, the force of forced couples such as Daphne and Apollo but not only them, also marriages, also Alzheimer's which forces Fraser's mother next to DeKooning in Fraser's mind and in the reader's, in the last section of the book called "A.D. Notebooks":

"the track of DeKooning's hand

the track of my
mother's hand"

—"notebook 7"[13]

Not the image that DeKooning's hand may have been making, not the impulse behind the gesture of her mother's hand tracking, but the space on the page between these two hands, the image between the images that are here composed of letters of words on the page, the image of the blank space between

Between
        "hand"
and
                "the"

Dedicated to the transmutation of the literal into the otherwise literal
sometimes named as it fleetingly passes:

"Do they see the gray animal shadow whizzing along the floorboards? Do they hear the parquet geometry of the wooden floor expanding, as if giving-up an hour of footsteps randomly wandering backwards, forwards?"

        —"You can hear her breathing" in
        "You can hear her breathing in the photograph"[14]

This naming of the fleetingly passing as one of the main necessities of this writing. Naming as a showing of the images between the images.

Nothing Happens

"…Ackerman's strategic indiscrimination between registers—the alternation between representation and abstraction in her minimal hyper-realist work… a dual ambition: to pursue what happens when nothing happens" could also be said, has also been said above, to be an ambition of *Discrete Categories*.[15]

extended duration, the thematics of the everyday. Who forces whom?
to couple, quadruple, quintuple
Perhaps much more than a "dual" ambition—an ever-increasing ambition and series of investigations into questions about the nature and origins of force.

The time of this air and/as rice. In this "uneventfulness" in which nothing happens: Air turns into rice and though that's not exactly nothing, it's also not a thing that can be measured or seen. Instead the duration of this passing, of this transmutation of something invisible, air, into something visible, rice, or letters falling down a page or sky, demonstrate the material nature of "unevenness." Unevenness and scattering through are in service of coming down, and together they alchemize and make an unnamed and unseeable object: duration, visible:

"…*words* as particles of matter in motion."[16]

Forced Questions

again a swerving laid out to any random viewer, in this case herself a cinematic event to which she would gradually attach herself as she drove forward and slowly shifted gears through the lengthening.[17]

In this passage an "anatomy of imagined capture" is exposed and imagined. Am I called to gradually "attach" myself as the "she" does? As a reader I try to imagine my options. Resist identification with the "she." Wonder if it would be a pleasure to attach myself to the "she" and thus become "any random viewer," and a "cinematic event" fueled by the forward motion of the car. Resist, whether a pleasure or not. The pleasure of resistance.

Barthes:

> the only linguistic approach to pleasure is, I believe, metaphor or more
> precisely catachresis: 'limping' metaphor in which the denoted term
> doesn't exist in language (the arms of a chair).
> …To speak not through adjectives but through
> metaphors, that is what poets used to do.[18]

to reveal that the metaphor is not metaphoric is, I think, what Fraser wants to do.

The arms of Barthes' chair, parallel here to the pleasure of the reader:
as if the chair could gesticulate
as if the reader has arms to choose with
as if the limp is someone else's

tension between writer insisting on pleasure
and reader not sure of the shackles of that, reiterates the thematic underbelly of
transmutation present throughout the book—the inability to turn into, being stuck or
stopped in motion—made to be static as a photo, statue, old story.

"She was inside and outside of him and visible, forced too soon by his definiteness.
Her indefiniteness was not tolerable to his practiced will."

—"You can hear her breathing"[19]

Translation, Transliteration, Transmutation, Trance

"I was stunned, for example, by the exact moment in a recent fictional work when a
woman notices her foot stepping up onto a curb and understands this to be an 'event.' It
was not so much the physical presence of the foot. No, that's wrong, it *was* the physical
presence (even though we are given no details, but at precisely the same time—as in both
sides of an equation—it was her knowing she knew, her discovering for herself the nature
of 'an event' or that this particular moment, or motion, had any importance at all to her

in a world of rain and cars...."

"...what had been the curb now became a screen with her foot projected onto it...."

—"Soft Pages"[20]

In discussing the Zukofskys' translations of Catullus, Hatlen says there is "...a rigorous fidelity to the line pattern of the original."[21]

Rather than a false parallel between Zukofsky and Fraser, I'm interested in Fraser's interest in this essay about Zukofsky and the kind of translations he and Celia did.

If *Discrete Categories* were a series of translations, the originals would be rain or traffic or thought interrupted by shoes or walking, instead of Catullus. And it could still be said that there is "a rigorous fidelity to the line pattern of the original." A rigorous discovery, not finished with the end of the book, of the nature of "an event."

"I like to read in the dark…"

When night comes I want to keep reading without turning on the light. In the future eyes will have adapted and some will be able to read in the dark. I envy them. I like to sit in the dark with many people I don't know. I can't wait till the lights go out. People are sitting in the dark reading together. The tall letters of words that would come up to your knees stop in front of you wavering slightly. Then someone turns the big invisible lever and the letters slowly disappear, line by line, swallowed up by the black mail slot under the screen. Still photos appear and hover for a full three minutes. Sometimes a grid of four photos, then later, a refrain, the same four again rearranged differently on the grid. And the voices too, separate elements falling over into sense, then rearranging themselves into storytelling, someone alone singing, and back again, running water, many feet on asphalt following the contours of how and where. Being sure, as Fallaci shows, that some people are responsible for setting it in motion more than others. Together we imagine it has taken place. More text that looks like an aerial view of heads in a piazza appears. A piazza because there is a fountain in the middle. The fountain of a capital O. And it is footprints in a square left by soldiers learning their marching formations. It is now creases in the sheet when your cheek is pressed against—when you are just waking into the reverse world. Inside of commentary what happened still happens. More. Again. Of what is this a document?—can always be asked but amnesia is the usual resort. Forgetfulness is entertainment. Is there any other way to crawl inside a book? Between document and event, commentary and reaction, put me between pages and close the door. This is a lullaby to wake you up. Of course it's the sleep of the visible secret that I want to see. The homecoming of the dead from the gulf war to the Dover Airforce Base in Delaware. Who has that footage?

◇◇◇◇◇◇

Oriana Fallaci, *Interview With History*, Thucydides, Herodotus, Salgado, Ondaatje, Zora Neale Hurston, Rhodessa Jones, Paul Rabinow, Vincent Crapanzano, Anna Devere Smith, Trinh T. Minh-ha, Michael Moore, Dorothy Richardson, Francis Ford Coppola, etc., etc.

Belief's Afterimage: The Recent Work of Barbara Guest

> A body by itself doesn't mean anything. You have to surround it with
> a story.
>
> —Vladimir Dzuro, Czech forensic detective[1]

> Body in the field—beyond uneven brick,
> *meaning in advance of itself.*
>
> —Barbara Guest, *If So, Tell Me*

Beginning again and again surrounding a body with story "another STORY BEGINS."[2]
Was there ever a body to begin with? Or can a body by itself exist? In Barbara Guest's
three recent books there is only surrounding—something imagined lying across the field of
the page beyond the uneven brick of type. Something in advance of meaning. Ship on fire
at open sea. Scene of a crime. Scene of a find.

To read Barbara Guest's three new books, almost simultaneously, is to visit a land of
elaboration. Due to the accident of their publication, all appearing in 1999 within a few
months of each other, *Rocks on a Platter*, *If So, Tell Me* and *The Confetti Trees* converse
more directly than they might if they had appeared further apart in time. Instead, I
(as many readers may have) read each all the way through then saw that by their own
momentum they began to shuffle—three decks of cards—doors to worlds so complex that
comment is paltry, leaving only the possibility of response. Although *The Confetti Trees*
was written long before the other two, it fully participates in the orbit of this trialogue.
Formally and otherwise the books are vastly different from each other and cannot be
conflated. But in the land which surfaces from the orbit of the three, Guest elaborates
a relation to language and writing that is more than "poetry" or a "poetics." It is an
interrogation of the structures of making, of meaning, and of the conduct of the writer in
writing, toward language.

In this land there are only the trappings of story. Story is a decoy that never does its
purported work of identifying the unmarked: "She submitted a few stories she called *The
Minus Ones*...."[3] Like the solitary body story is always minus, always hungry. σπαραγμός—

ritual dismemberment—the body by itself is ecstatic, flying to pieces, marvelous in its occupation of the place no story can fully enter.[4] Here in this crevice, death palace, where the decay of story's function is revealed, the writing takes place:

> *Now* the pain has left the body. Only an outline remains. Down by the bathhouse where the soundless waves tumble the *Montage* ends in an unfinished tree. Nothing is alive. A writer sits at *Windows*, a woman on his Screen. He puts her on a reef with the shipwrecked sailor. The feeble sun he paws will not burn.

> —"Nostalgia," *Confetti Trees*[5]

The problem of making the body mean, burn, is always present in this work—the body as the form, the outline, the music of the writing—comes into being, like the blood or thought of a flesh body, as part of breathing, not prior or in opposition to breath; not as if words were mere content or subject, but letter by letter, syllable by syllable, line break by line, the body of the poem proposes itself, becomes a burning organism or not. And the subject of Guest's writing is often also the conditions of this becoming. In the above poem she suggests that the conditions of each making differ depending on who proposes them, and by what means they are enacted. This time a *he* sits at a (computer, or film, or dream, or TV) screen looking out its windows into the Screen. "A writer" thinks he is writing—thinks he is producing something alive. In "his" screen he sees a woman who he thinks is not a reflection of himself. But Guest tells that "Nothing is alive" in this "Montage" and he confuses his reflection for a screen woman, or thinks the screen woman is alive—He "puts" or writes the screen woman "on a reef"—an order of looking, of fantasy, of reflecting, a putting as order that produces "A writer" or writing in which the "the feeble sun he paws will not burn."

Throughout the three books, Guest investigates the conditions, the various means of burning, of producing illumination—by reflection, a trick of mirrors, or by candle, computer, lamp, cigarette, film projector—each from a different era and producing different effects in the hands of different operators—poets, philosophers, composers, among others—rifling through her effects. In the above poem "Nostalgia," Guest makes a nostalgia that replaces the proposition of *happened* with the act of *told*. Nostalgia becomes not a longing for what happened but a desire to investigate how what happened was told. If there is no actual event, only telling, only writing, then how it was told is what happened. Each of the three books returns to an investigation into the conditions of illumination which is also an investigation into the conditions of telling. As a detective might return to the scene of a crime in order to discover what happened—here, where there is "Only an outline" the "remains"—Guest gives clues of story as memory of that which may never have occurred but like fantasy, like the symbolic order, continues to impact us. Here the alive poem reports on, builds a place in which nothing is alive, but the poem itself is burning. Thus "Nothing is alive" takes us to the unsurrounded body, imagination itself—where everything is animate, even things that may not appear to be

> They told her they liked real fires and not those of the imagination.
> Imagination was harmful and always messed up the set.
>
> —"The Minus Ones,"[6]

Putting burning where the props and plot were on the set, Guest harms the set, Strikes it, replacing, stripping, what appears to be intact. Writing as an act of removal—exhuming the body to reveal—unravel the story to keep the furniture, the food cooking on the stove, while removing the walls of the house. Use the utensils, the elements, the structures of myth, poetry, fairytale, screenplay, narrative, to expose the beams and bolts. To require that we listen inside-out and doubly. Surround the body with subtraction since the body is always already cloaked in story as before it is born it is clothed in a history. That which is made up and can never fully reveal the origins of it's making.

> That which shows itself and at the same time withdraws is the essential trait of what we call the mystery. I call the comportment which enables us to keep open to the meaning hidden in technology, *openness to the mystery*.
>
> —Heidegger[7]

In all three books "openness to the mystery" is Guest's comportment—mystery is also a word she uses in "Mysteriously Defining the Mysterious," a talk given in 1986 about poetry. Guest's mode of accessing Heidegger's "meaning hidden in technology" is through a technology of writing in which the word *make* is as important as the word *meaning* since the mode of making, the technology and the meaning are inseparable, are the same. A writing repeatedly emerges that is *techne* about and of *techne*, mysterious but not mystifying: writing as finger on the disappearing present body of writing writer, of writing writing.

White

perpendicular lights   attached to the shoulder
I touched the wrist with my writing finger   and from the center
the orb of the eye was enough fire   to light the writing lamp and
afterwards   the blade   withdrew from the writing shoulder   and
that writ
blew away   flame lit with nothing   and nothingness stayed

      Skin of the lost paper
          Knuckle smooth   (touched the writing).

        Nietzschean   thumb on
                  the trout
           and they disappear.

—Rocks on a Platter[8]

Technology's *techne*, the machinations, writing finger's methods of making, chosen, as it were live on camera, while pawing a "feeble sun," or at gunpoint, that is, in the face of the urgency of "poetry of the moment" a "flame lit with nothing   and nothingness stayed."[9] Each moment approaching nothing because: "In whatever guise reality becomes visible, the poet withdraws from it into invisibility."[10]

This writing that invokes the apparition of nothing, as if to make the invisible visible—a practice, a technique of deception which makes encounter:

practices of deception existing: to encounter   arm, and sun,
cloak   did not have its own ambition until they *vanish and*
return

Meaning, also.

                              —"Deception"[11]

Through this (writing) deception, things discover their "own ambition" which is the
ambition, desire, of the poem. Practicing techniques of deception in order to create
encounter which can only be *vanish and return*—what appears to be the light of day is
"sun, cloak…." Revealing and concealing meaning, Guest requires that we listen doubly,
duplicitly, quadruply, to mystery, day's ambition, the light of night, illuminating "This
elaborate structure around the text."[12] Thus the three books confound distinctions,
particularly that between poetry and poetics, making *comportment* more useful in thinking
about them than *poetics*. A comportment toward language, the mystery. A practice of
approach, that is, of writing, "which expresses 'yes' and at the same time 'no,' [named]
by an old word, *releasement toward things.*"[13] The release of meaning to its own life
beyond what is meant "Moves outside the text into the dark *under text*…."[14] Meaning
that disregards genre or answer except where useful as toy takes instead "repercussions,
soundings"—music of thinking or conversations across time, replace explanation or telling,
though the vehicles, demonstrations and sounds of it differ. "We once took a ship"—
listen "royal traveler"—is your name "dissonance"? Is it Schoenberg? Nietzsche? Walser?
Richardson? Spenser? Husserl, H.D., Hegel, Chaucer, Heidegger, Adorno, Coleridge,
Hölderlin? "To whom and with who else is this address?" This is decay's deportment: place
of story without story begging and undoing story

            Skin of the lost paper
               Knuckle smooth   (touched the writing)

Conjuring an ethnographically "real" Hollywood of World War II in *The Confetti Trees*,
Guest uses the film camera to demonstrate exactly the ways in which "practices of
deception" can illuminate more than "realistic" documentation or plot ever can. As they
do in the desire to enter an ideal world of the made, displaced by the entrance into the
motion of motion picture:

            The action began in heavy mechanical studio rain. An actor in a brown overcoat
            lit a cigarette and detaching himself from the group entered the house. Other

110

actors in brown overcoats with lit or unlit cigarettes entered the house. One by one as the director watched, the actors reappeared. Each carried a barrel he then pushed down the rickety steps of the house.

One more detail decided the Director. Over his loud speaker he called to the actors to put out their cigarettes. "No smokes! Not in this rain! Keep the unlit cigarettes in your mouths. Keep pushing the barrels! In and out of the house more and more barrels! Four more times. Before the real storm hits."

…He lived in the real world too much these days. He hated reality. His raincoat had already dampened the seat of his expensive car and there were puddles on the floor. Puddles! In his beautiful car! That was what was wrong. You had no control over reality. He sat back in his seat, prepared to reconsider the film in terms of an apparition with absolutely no intrusion of the physical world and its weather.

—"Details"[15]

The action begins in doubleness that is likeness. The sublimated "physical" of the physical world. "…heavy mechanical studio rain," and "Puddles!"—"lit" and "unlit cigarettes" requiring further investigation into the nature of semblance:

> She shall disclose herself (herself still pointing)
>   essential to the hidden
>
> possessiveness in back of a throat,
>
>   *the double* S *of the word*.
>
> —"Deception"[16]

herself   herself

the double d

of hidden

and the lower and uppercase

d of Director

As in

　　"A likeness   to what is believed

is the poem. The camera takes us, momentarily."

　　　　　—"annunziare!"[17]

Just like what you believe is a world of proposed beliefs, but the poem is not itself what you believe—and likeness not where you would expect: *Rocks on a Platter* the "poetics" book is poetry about poetry, philosophy, reading, etc., no more or less than the other two are *Rocks*' subtitle: "Notes on Literature." In this land there can be no ideal Platonic form of poetics or the poem "outside" the poem that occupies a realm of belief. In advance of meaning or behind it—the apparition, acts of this particular comportment are what one can believe and the poem is belief's afterimage. "Yet this demise…"—of belief? of the poem? of the soul proposed as "an actor in a brown overcoat" lighting a cigarette? putting out a cigarette?—"…shows itself in fragments, just as the poet slowly dies in his or her poem making sure there are fragments remaining of the empire which created the poem, the empire of the poet's soul."[18]

Errant Alphabet: Notes Toward the Screen

Last spring I curated an event called "Between Screen and Page: the Motion of the Written Seen." All of the work shown used text on screen. SILT, a film collective, Elise Hurwitz, a filmmaker, and Fanny Howe, a filmmaker poet, showed and talked about their work. While it is impossible to summarize all that propelled this event into existence, a few of the thoughts, questions, and quotes that return in thinking about the relations between the screen and page follow:

—First, neither are blank—ever—they arrive already written upon

—The meaning of the image can never be contained within its borders. On page and screen then it's the excess beyond itself, that which is not itself, beyond the frame— wherever that may be—which generates meanings

—As Barthes says, the distinction between still and moving image does not hold once the image is analyzed as a dynamic of inside/outside relations

—Do films and videos that have letters written in/on them confound the sense of there being an inside and outside of the film?

—Does writing that requires a filmic reading of itself also confound that sense of the page being a static limiting frame? And what are the structures that make a writing be read "filmically"?

—Does writing on and around film complicate conventions of reading? If the visual is a dominant mode of representation, does writing on the film complicate models of truth based on the dominance of the visual?

—Eisenstein talked of the film as a writing machine…

—Can words on paper be a motion picture machine?

—The dream and the hieroglyph—especially useful since both resist any reduction to the purely visible…

—When writing appears on screen—does the film become, like a dream or hieroglyph, impossible to reduce to the purely visible or purely scriptural?

—Is that also what happens when a ruptured word or letter appears on screen? And/Or even if a word appears on screen intact does putting it on screen simulate rupture or force it to actually be ruptured?

—Are there any literal parallels that can be made when working simultaneously between film, video and writing? For example in composing on the page one might consider line breaks, rhythm, punctuation, lyric, echo, ellipses, etc.

—When one composes film, or takes writing on paper and puts it on screen, can the frame be thought of as a unit of punctuation, an edit as a line break, a track shot as ellipses, or…?

—"In analyzing the inside/outside frame one is incessantly reminded of the past and the past is a specter, the past is death."—Peter Brunette and David Wills, *Screen/Play: Derrida and Film Theory*

—Which leads to the mother, her body, source of mortality, all that the mother's body invokes: the erotic desire to get as close as possible to the screen (which isn't actually anywhere) in order to see oneself, to become a self, to die together—which is what viewing in the dark can be like, can trigger….

At the event I passed out the following sheet of quotes:

March 29, 1996

BETWEEN SCREEN AND PAGE: THE MOTION OF THE WRITTEN SEEN

+ The film is a social art, a show, something for collective seeing, and even in the day that finds us all owning projectors and rolls of film from the circulating filmery it still will be so, a small ceremonial prepared for a group, all of whom must adjust their sensibilities at a

given moment and at the film's pace. Reading, all but reading aloud, is a solitary art... — and the film can no more replace it than the Mass can replace private devotions. The film is skyey apparition, white searchlight. The book remains the intimate, domestic friend, the golden lamp at the elbow.
—Dorothy Richardson, "Continuous Performance: Almost Persuaded," *Close Up* (June 1929), 34.

+ I am for—no illustration; everything a book evokes should happen in the reader's mind: but, if you replace photography, why not go straight to cinematography, whose successive unrolling will replace, in both pictures and text, many a volume, advantageously....
Mallarmé, in response to a questionnaire, quoted by Jacques Derrida in "The Double Session," *Dissemination*, trans. Barbara Johnson (Chicago: University of Chicago Press, 1981), 208.

+ ...to the extent that it is a language, it [film] is to be considered as a type of writing.
—Peter Brunette and David Wills, *Screen/Play: Derrida and Film Theory* (Princeton, New Jersey: Princeton University Press, 1989), 61.

+ The spatial problems of film editing, framing and making are also narrative ones because ...frame space is constructed as narrative space.
—Stephen Heath, *Questions of Cinema* (London: Macmillan, 1981), 38.

+ It is all the more interesting to come back to the point when this model [that of 'classical narrative'] wavers—in order to detect the privileged fracture zones, and in particular to define the remarkable relationships forming between the activity of writing, conceived of as the hieroglyphic form of editing, and written representation.
—Marie Claire Ropars, "The Graphic in Filmic Writing: *À bout de souffle*, Or The Erratic Alphabet," *Enclitic* 5, 2/6, no. 1 (1981–82): 147–61.

+ The shot can be considered as a unit of writing to the extent that it challenges any claim made by sense to constitute its units....
—*Screen/Play*, 134.

+ ...the heterogeneity of elements [in *À bout de souffle*, or *Breathless* in English] implies

a very complex system of competing forces, of plays of power, and she [Ropars] finds…
that the "radical potentiality" of the registers of cited texts and image/sound relations, is
"superintended" by relations of sexual difference that control "the dissemination of letters
in the film."
—*Screen/Play*, 132; and as discussed by David Rodowick in "The Figure and the Text,"
Diacritics 15/1 (Spring 1985): 34–50.

+ The hieroglyph hypothesis… that has been reinforced by the film's paragrammatic
density, the editing's ability to make the alphabet err into protean anagrams: when
scriptural activity gets intense, we have seen the title and meaning come undone, and we
have circulated fragments thus taken up from language along multiple channels—iconic or
verbal, literal or vocal.
—Ropars, "The Graphic in Filmic Writing," 158. [*Breathless* is the film referred to here.]

+ …as if the image launched desire beyond what it permits us to see.
—Roland Barthes, *Camera Lucida: Reflections on Photography*, trans. Richard Howard (New
York: Hill and Wang, 1981), 59.

+ Anthony Fragola: What is it that film can accomplish that the written work cannot?
There must be something intrinsic to film that draws you to it. What is there in film that
allows you to express what you want to express?
Alain Robbe-Grillet: There is *nothing* I want to express. I have *nothing* to express.
Roch Smith: What pleases you in the manipulation of cinematographic forms? The
manipulation of images, or—A. R.-G:—images and sounds…. I have nothing at all to
express that *precedes* expression….
…Since I am interested in the narrative, cinema is for me a way of practicing narrative
without making use of words…. I am primarily interested in images and sounds. Dialogue
is not useless, but it is only one specific element…. For me, it is really a question of the
structures of images, structures of montage, and structures of sound. With words also, but
they function only as one, nonprivileged element —not at all privileged, as a matter of
fact.
—Anthony Fragola and Roch Smith, *The Erotic Dream Machine: Interviews with Alain
Robbe-Grillet on His Film* (Carbondale and Edwardsville: Southern Illinois University Press,
1992), 146–148.

+ A film is like a page of paper which I offer the viewer.
—Trinh T. Minh-ha, *Framer Framed* (New York: Routledge, 1992), 173.

◇◇◇◇◇◇

I grew up in Los Angeles and spent much of my childhood on the Universal Studios lot. My grandfather was the head of the music department at Universal. Many hours passed as I sat on his lap while he conducted an orchestra and simultaneously scored the music for a movie playing in front of us. Afterwards we would walk around the lot looking at one set after another. I was fascinated by the real rowboat floating on painted water, the sunlight cast by a lamp, and other such sights that unhinged any sense of the "real" world off the Universal lot being a stable place, or of movies being any less "real" than life off screen. This early exposure to the gap between the representation and the thing being represented, indeed the question of whether there ever *is* a stable thing that can be represented by any representation, has permeated my relation to language. Thus in my writing I am preoccupied, for example, by questions about the function of the page as a screen, and the function of reference as an effect to be investigated and dismantled as one might take apart a movie set.

◇◇◇◇◇◇

SET

Everywhere action and no motion
seizure, no body
sentence no subtitle
afterlife, no limbs
afterlight—all caption

—from "Black Box Cutaway"

(San Francisco, 1996)

117

Motion Picture Home

PROGRAM NOTES, with an excerpt from the play *Motion Picture Home*

Motion Picture Home is a play that is an interrogation of the question of what a play is—of what a play enacts—does or can do—even what the dimensional physical world can do and does—it and worlds that seem not to be dimensional, physical.

It performs a refusal, or rehearsal, or inability to perform—An interrogation also of the notion of performance—where does it take place? Where is the stage and what can an audience expect to witness there? What is the use of the living person on stage?—Of living in theatre? If almost nothing "happens" on the stage, where might that nothing propose that living happening does occur? What is *happening*?

If the performers and audience are as much "listeners" as seers, then the spectacle of an audience, being confronted with, included in, the problems of a play, an interrogation of its conditions, as the substance of the play—in addition to an ongoing dialogue of interrogation—becomes the noise of mind, of minds at work, as the *action* of the play, a play—Is this what happening *is*?

MPH engages death, decision, perseveration, conflict, the face of possibility, thwarted possibility, the tension between speech and speaking, and the question of the bridgeable or unbridgeable gap between speech and action, speech as action—The question of what intention has to do with executed action, if anything—And the proposition that motion is equivalent to being alive—And so asks: what then does *alive* look and sound like on what stage? Do plays usually enact the alive? Is poetry as play, at play, the way life recognizes, runs into itself, on this or that scene of intention? What is a play that demonstrates, mimics, performs, motion? Does that play require human bodies?

What does language without action—without correspondence in the 3-D world—not as one to one reference—but as action in itself, look and sound like? The language that is not about life, but is, itself, life, alive—is in a sense not in need of a stage, *is* simultaneously stage's place and action. Then the 3-D becomes a redundancy—but sometimes redundant in the most fascinating sense: that words and thought be simultaneously translated in object and gesture—that the boundaries between word, object and gesture break and duplicate—be witnessed in the act of breaking down and repeating. That the words of object and gesture make a fabulous show of redundancy, a cacophonous cocoon of thought-life, multiplied to the infinite power—That would be *Motion Picture Home*'s hope.

> Finally but most importantly, the material aspects of its equipment and the intellectual aspects of its performances are in the closest possible connection with the interests of the listener. What kind of power can the theatre generate by comparison [to radio]? The use of a living medium and nothing else. Perhaps the situation of the theatre has been led into a crisis in which no question is as important as the following one: What can be said about the use of the living person in theatre?
>
> —Walter Benjamin[1]

New Langton Arts, San Francisco
(February 9, 2002)

Excerpt MOTION PICTURE HOME

In the play:
—Voice-over #1, 2, 3 and 4 [*some voice-overs are live but delivered from off stage, some are recorded; live voice-over #1 is the same person as recorded voice-over #1, etc.…*]
—Teleprompter: as a character in live and recorded voice-over—And—an actual teleprompter machine present on stage operated (off stage) by a professional teleprompteress
—Time Lord, Sir Sanford Flemming, inventor of standardized time, English accent
—Woman
—The Little Dog

The script is read at a fast clip
Otherwise the play is spoken live off stage, with the exception of the "Woman" character that occasionally speaks when on stage.

First it is only dark on stage. Then, the teleprompter comes on and scrolls these words on its monitor screen:

> And all the motion came home and
> all the moving parts came to rest

Stage lights come up and the set can be seen: a big TV monitor sits near the back and a slide of a big touch-tone phone keypad is projected on back wall. Sound of TV static— channel gone off air. Teleprompter to side of stage.

Voice-over 1:
(*with static still on*): Was that the final time?
Voice-over 2:
No, rest keeps refusing to be final; keeps being interrupted

V1:
I want to see rest. Can you make it visible?
V2:
As visible as
V1:
You're too hungry for action
V2:
It's like an anorexia for motion
V1:
Get dressed
V2:
Orders?
V1:
All dialogue is assignments.
V2:

So you expect me to respond? [*Pause*]

Listen. I know how to shut you up

V1:

Tell me everything

V2:

You might think I am; you will expect to see something, as usual. You will think I'm giving you something to see.

V1:

Now get ready for bed!

Teleprompter:

[*slightly mocking and sing-song tone*]
Come on get dressed, get ready for bed, put on your rain boots. Not orders—schedules, itineraries—this is how the train runs, this is how the water boils
This is how I, the Teleprompter, tell and tell and tell and tell

[*Pause, TV static stops, then teleprompter voice continues in a different neutral narrating tone*]
She lives in a house near the sea. She goes into it. The air is warm. One man lives there but is never

[*V1 and V2 begin reading the play again here on top of the following narration. Each time the "Woman" character and Voice-over 3 speak, a line from the first part of the play is read almost on top of the following "story" narration. The volume of the reading by V1 and V2 of the 1st part of the play varies. Sometimes all of the story narration is run over in this way; sometimes the timing is different and only parts of it are. STOP will indicate when this interrupted narrating ends*]
…home. Three women are in the house when she comes back.

Woman:

[*walks on to stage, carrying a pile of too many things in her arms: rubber gloves, glass figurines, long florescent light bulb tubes, Morton salt, masking tape, bicycle pedals, tools, machine parts—looking at the slide on back wall of stage says:*]
I am not happy at their presence

[She begins to make a pile of rubble out of the things that were in her arms. Begins to work with salt]

Voice-over 3:

She searches the house with her eyes to see what could be violated by them. A partially open drawer full of shreds of curled purple paper presents the first possibility. She says to herself

Woman:

It's purple cabbage

V3:

Do you remember what to do with it?

Woman:

Take a fistful and put it on a table. Take out the musical score paper.
[She takes one strand at a time and places it carefully on the bars. Then when the strands are arranged they merge with the paper and become music which she can hear or they turn into flat words on the bars of the paper.]
I look back at the three women. They are squabbling with each other

V1:

Each starts reprimanding and yelling. She yells back

Woman:

Get out! Get out!

V2:

They begin to cower and leave

Woman:

I follow them out into the dirt street and keep yelling "Go away!"

[STOP]

[Pause, as if watching the distance]
They begin to diminish, their postures curve, they age before my eyes, they turn their backs and hurry down the street
[Muttering as she leaves the stage:]

Fates? Muses? Musketeers? Mutations?

Teleprompter:

Stop interrupting! I mean interpreting!

V3:

Or what about the one called "House Full of Crickets"?
Or "The Grandmother on a stage?" No,

V1:

Preappearance it goes from name to name
Who does the dream target? Who forget?
Seal your account book and leave it on the ground
something must have before
the year mill
this is only and merely
grinding called passing
But still I miss remembering
a series of familiar but unknown that are my
The field comes up to meet a plate of lake
rises
the mirror
face on hinges
Flashlight life

V2:

I now want actors to act, make a gesture of speech that divides air! Now photograph my
mouth up close, like dental work, now turn it into sound!

[*Same voice shifting to a lower, quieter more gentle and seductive tone:*]
I want to go right through our autism to become an actual object. Then our eastern
European ancestors will wake up from their cult-of-the-child sleep. Finally to touch each
other. We could have siesta sleeping together one afternoon over the phone.

[*Normal more neutral tone again:*]
The characters all want me to work for them. I am their whore, but even though they

pay me I have to seduce them to let me work. Then they make sudden appearances and disappearances at whim, like a father waving good-by before going out for a death bike ride—all so casual that the mundane and the extraordinary shake hands canceling each other out. Let them work for themselves for once!

[*While the Teleprompter talks the woman goes on to the stage and turns the TV on. Sound of static starts up again*]

Teleprompter:

You have a name but that is not enough to be a character

How could you fall asleep when you were suppose to be building the diorama
I mean watching the kids
[*Pause*]
In brackets, as if written by the other author who is reading: "I am second-sight impaired, thought the author"—Hélène Cixous.
Scorched garden. Burnt offering. The beginning. No. Burnt garden. Scorched sun. Offering no beginning. Digging here in the ashes the only starting, starling, startling. What I have left of you: a stone from the path where you fell. Perfect for your chest. But your burial was not yours, or ours—burial of complicity, someone else's wish disguised as second guess

V3:

[*Coyly,* like telling a secret about stealing:]
Confiscation. I am confiscation.

V1:

Break and enter broken and entered
The dark of broad daylight. You all want to steal it for your story...

(2002)

Outer Event

Three Desks

Myung Mi Kim said, "Let's make lists of all of our discursive writing and look at those lists." I began a list soon lost under piles. In the intervening years the bit of edification, the muzzle, gag and tethers of training that determined much of what fell to that list have remained of interest while the sign of the "discursive" under which the list accreted has become increasingly perplexing.

There are daily occasions that provoke response or invitations that require address. Vigilant against the learned behavior of automatic response yet immersed also in a porous need-world in which adrenaline calls the mother, whether or not she has children, before or after, to tend to the call.

> The call is not the song. The Latin *obaudire*, hearing from below—obeying.
>
> —George Albon

Here enter the imaginal and actual laws that authorize kinds of public discourse by kinds of public bodies. The bit and muzzle and their company surface at the moment of the call, as if address requires some kind of redress too: obedience. The writing that escapes seems to be poetry.

Years ago, unable to confine myself to the dissertation writing at the computer on my desk, I put a table to my right and another behind me. The one to the side was a repository for writing related to the topics of the dissertation but occurring in an idiolect different from that of the academy. What I recognized as poetry, sometimes related to the dissertation topics and sometimes not, fell to the third table behind me.

Starting before the occupation of the dissertation chamber and continuing long after that triangulation, an attempt to repeatedly take resistance and desire, to write not only about them, not issue only from them, and also not ignore them.

I am interested in what prompts and makes possible this process of entering what one is estranged from—and in what disables the foray.

—Toni Morrison*

Perhaps for some an academic discourse is native, without ambivalence, or easy to learn. For me it was none of those.

Help arrived as the learning and re-learning, the consecutive and simultaneous ordering and disassembling of one posture after another—perhaps a brain patterning via the body?—of the t'ai chi form:

Question 4: To withdraw is then to release, to release is to withdraw... but what is "in discontinuity there is still continuity"?

Answer: Discontinuity is the physical form and continuity is the *i* (mind). It is like a broken lotus root with the fibers still connected. In Chinese calligraphy the stroke may be broken, but the mind is still connected.

—*T'ai Chi Classics*

T'ai chi arrived as a kind of third apprehension: not poetry, not academic discourse—but linking and partaking of some of both of these, and more. An embodied instruction in sequence and phrase that is and is not sequential. No surprise when you think of the Greek for discourse invoking the body in the act of twice bringing or throwing the discus, thus as a measure, like foot size, *diskoura*, διόκουρα, of distance. Or if you listen to the many contradictory definitions for the word *discourse* in the O.E.D., some excoriating, some invoking the body and the household. Or think of *dissakis*, διοσάκις, *poet., adv.,* *twice over.*

That worked and later unworked—*re-broken lotus root with the fibers still connected*—writing that became the dissertation, later became a book—not *of*—but partaking of poetry. The hope to address the requirement and desire to learn a particular vocabulary, taxonomy and comportment of thinking and speaking with its rules of inclusion and exclusion and to simultaneously consider the valences of silence and other kinds of thinking and utterance—these efforts to practice forms of *discontinuity in continuity* continued beyond the three desk scene. Training to become an academic or a car mechanic or a ten-year-old cotillion dancer requires practice in particular etiquette, ethics and manners. Usually training to become a specialist makes one a specialist in correct etiquette. Once in a while someone also becomes thoughtful and curious, or a bacchic dancer within or beyond the waltz.

WHAT IS IT YOU HAVE COME TO TELL ME?

> Ultimately, the good reason of our refusal to censor or to "correct" is that we seek not to get rid of what embarrasses us or what does not seem true to our lights but to go beyond embarrassment—beyond shame or disgust or outrage —to imagine in an other light, to see in a larger sight what we had rather was dismissed from view.

> —Robert Duncan

We might wish for a fugitive writing but all writing, including poetry, must contend in some way with the reign of the discursive—even if only to attempt to ignore or subvert its rule.

> Yet maybe this institution and this inclination are but two converse responses to the same anxiety: anxiety as to just what discourse is when it is manifested materially, as a written or spoken object.

> —Michel Foucault**

In the realm of our current academic or medical or legal discursives, in which "proceeding by reasoning or argument" is the prevailing use of the word, one who refuses or is unable to be trained to tolerate the rigors of correction, the bit of edification, is often viewed as deficient—or she is regaled as a "real" Poet, having "escaped" via a royal road called "inspiration." This divide we inherit and in which we live takes me back to one of its origins in the *Ion*: "…for not by art does the poet sing but by power divine… God takes away the minds of poets…." The current discursive trains for meaning minus exhilaration.

Thinking minus music.

> Poetry and music are both patterns of sound drawn on a background of time....
> Whatever refinements and subtleties they may introduce, if they lose touch
> altogether with the simplicity of the dance, with the motions of the human body
> and the sounds natural to a man exerting himself, people will no longer feel
> them as music and poetry. They will respond to them, no doubt but not with the
> exhilaration that dancing brings.

> —Basil Bunting

We could think of poetry and music as elements of a kind of thought that involves voices
issuing from bodies in motion. A sequence of actions, something like a dance or embodied
incantation. Each step across the page might propose a measure of distance. A foot equals
a sound unit or sentence. Invitation to a choreography of relation—the proximity of
bodies—in a room doing the t'ai chi form—a call, body to body, like seaweed waving
to currents in the air, or following the space of the page before word, each posture a
hexagram, a sequence taking letter shapes—a form of thought and address—

What is it you have come to tell me?

Address

In the difficulty, there is no other to address but address itself.

If I could begin this is where I would begin.

Investigating these gags and tethers that attempt to keep us from violating the conventions of discursive utterance. That is investigating what we think we know about what thinking looks and sounds like—and should—this is the labor of a reflexive and reflective discourse.

> All research is crisis. What is sought is nothing other than the turn of seeking, of research, that occasions this crisis: the critical turn.
>
> —Maurice Blanchot

The turning back to look—to have recourse—does not turn one into a salt pillar

Looking at the curse as it has been inherited through the social and the family over generations, as in, "You made my grandfather eat his children in a stew [Pelops] and therefore I will now kill you in revenge" and on and on for generations of blood-letting. Discourse as a kind of revenge, inheritance, heritage of bloodletting, that occurs in some academic and other cultural conventions, under the sign of which, the slaughter of what came before, one kind of looking back, is recognizable as the work of correction and improvement called contribution to the present.

Is there a way to talk, read, write, within the social fabric, canon, family, without continuing blood feud?—Is there a course that doesn't lead, as it did for the Erinyes, Medea, Antigone, etc., to the punishment and shelter of the law of the polis? The banishment of the speech of the Furies to the hearth safely imprisoned inside the house?

The crisis of "the critical turn" is always present and always collapsing response, call, poetry, criticism, event, recollection. Always looking back at that second of a death, an origin, an invitation.

Marcel said they were incapable of establishing priorities. In fact their priorities were simply different priorities: value was assigned to all events equally but serially; what was going on at the moment—Aziz's [murder] trial, a stray chicken—had top billing. Neither event would have a lasting hold on them. Special fondness was attached to those incidents and persons with the greatest dramatic possibilities—that is, with a continuing, endlessly repeatable and improvable life in the imagination: memory of a kind.

—Isabel Fonseca

In place of subordination, imagination. Like incantation—not without cause and effect as one can repeat one thing and something else may occur as a result. One could engage a telling memory of the remembered unfolding present that prioritizes that of "greatest dramatic possibility" and enacts the critical turn as ratiocination of a kind. Lyric might be of high priority in a response to the continual crisis of seeking.

Lyric has no sound but recalls sound… The way a promise is an action made in speech, not in the sense of something scriptable or repeatable, but something that "happens," that "occurs" as an event and can continually be called upon… in the unfolding present.

—Susan Stewart

At that second of the sound of the call, writing poetry is a promise that involves the desolation of the impossible charge. The enactment of a coherent public face that the discursive seems to demand puts me in a different state of desolation.

I am no doubt not the only one who writes in order to have no face.

—Michel Foucault

In some poetry the writer dwells on the desolation wire of the impossibility of writing within/while writing. Passing from premises to conclusions in the discursive mode we are taught to act, to masquerade as if writing is possible—without obstacle, as if we are not our own obstacle—as if the assignment to convey meaning, argument, language as tool in service of that, can be met.

Is the desolation wire the phatic place where the song eclipses, overshadows, devours, extends beyond the call? Phatic as in *phanein*, φᾰνερός, to show, to appear visible,—even if in disguise. Does, can a wounded and double-faced, doubt-filled, unfaithful to orders, faceless, full frontal critical writing exist?

If it could, would we be able then to burn the need for the distinction between the discursive, and other writing?

> What is always at work in discourse—as in everything else—is desire and power.... This is why discourse, at least since the rout of the Sophists by Plato, always unfolds in the service of the "will to truth." Discourse wishes "to speak the truth." But in order to do this, it must mask from itself its service to desire and power, must indeed mask from itself the fact that it is itself a manifestation of the operations of these two forces.
>
> —Hayden White

Whose "truth" does which discourse wish us to speak, to serve up, to write?

Third Apprehension

All reasoning is carried on discursively; that is discurrendo,—by running about to the right and the left, laying the separate notices together, and thence mediately deriving some third apprehension.

—*O.E.D.*

Plucking from the definitions which themselves are laden with so much contradiction: invoking the inherent of the incoherent

…A subject of 'discourse' or reasoning (as distinguished from a subject of perception)

—*O.E.D.*

Perception as a kind of reason?
To lift the ancestral curse from this House of Atreus and turn it on itself.

Here the reflective recursive appears as the chorus that provides "another side to… conception," even another kind of conception

And, of course, s/he might begin with the writing. S/he might try to put the whole *dialogue* in new writing, the field of another kind of voice than those we have heard before. A help-ful, in-forming voice, a voice eager to reach and accept the other's voice. Already in chorus, or eager to reach for chorus. It might get started like that. Any day, it could begin like that. Any day it could begin.

—Nathaniel Tarn

The intolerable restrictions of the drama could be loosened, however, if a means could be found by which what was general and poetic, comment, not action, could be freed without interrupting the movement of the whole. It is this that the choruses supply; the old men or women who take no active part in the drama,

132

the undifferentiated voices who sing like birds in the pauses of the wind; who can comment, or sum up, or allow the poet to speak himself or supply, by contrast, another side to his conception.

— Virginia Woolf

As legend has it the first actor, the "hypocrit," was Thespis, the first to appear on stage as a "character" of a written play instead of as "himself," as a writer. He was also the first to exchange words with the leader of the chorus. The ὑποκρῐτής, the hypocrit could be enlisted to appear on our current discursive stage as the figure who addresses and provokes "the undifferentiated voices who sing like birds in the pauses of the wind; who can comment, or sum up, or allow the poet to speak himself or supply, by contrast, another side to his conception." Hypocrit from *ηypokrisia, ὑποκρῐσία—of stringed instruments, answer in sound, i.e. sound in harmony with, to play an accompaniment.* This hypocrit, being (at least) two-faced, could begin to "in-form" as Tarn suggests, begin to reach for a chorus that has already begun, to seduce and aggravate that chorus into more comment, summary, and more sides to conception.

The hypocrit talks with the chorus who talks to the audience. They all need each other to stay with/in the play. When the reader talks with the writer, is the reader the hypocrit or the chorus or the audience? The performance by all involves answering, harmonizing, assessing, contradicting: in short, interpretation—critical turns, a turning into, and turning from and toward heard and written passages.

> One must be able to pass easily into those ecstasies, those wild and apparently irrelevant utterances, those sometimes obvious and commonplace statements, to decide their relevance or irrelevance, and give them their relation to the play as a whole.

> We must be able to 'pass easily'; but that of course is exactly what we cannot do.... But we can guess that Sophocles used them not to express something outside the action of the play, but to sing the praises of some virtue, or the beauties of some place mentioned in it.

> —Virginia Woolf

It might not be possible or desirable to resuscitate, reconstitute or intervene in the orders of the discursive under whose reign we live, but it could be possible instead to enlist it, turn it into, turn to it as a recursive chorus that doesn't express something "outside the action of the play," (or the poem, or thinking) but reflects on and joins in singing "the praises of some virtue, or the beauties of some place mentioned in it" and examines its ethics and aesthetics, in order "to decide their relevance or irrelevance, and give them their relation to the play." And we could ask the hypocrit to digress from the narrative, as the aria singer does, to invite the pets, the gospel mass choir, the recitative, the dolphins and circadae who comment on us and make a place (chorus also invoking an enclosed place, χόρτος, a feeding place, a farmyard in which cattle were kept) between speech, song, premise, conclusion, thought and law.

This recursive chorus would not be performing a meta-function of poetry, as poetry is always in "the play as a whole." A whole? Where is the inside or outside of the play? Why do we even need to call this writing that enlists the wounded, double-faced, doubt-filled and faceless, something other than poetry? I think that is because we cannot ignore or pretend that we do not still live under the Pythagorean. And in the territory of address of the upper class, male only citizens, playwrights, actors and members of the chorus.

> DUALISM: Under the good the Pythagoreans ranged light, unity, understanding, rest, the straight, male, right, definite, even, and square; and under evil as contraries, darkness, plurality, opinion, movement, the curved, female, left, indefinite, odd, irregular.
> Promethean aspiration: To be a woman and a Pythagorean feminine. I go in disguise. Signification, Soul under stress, thread of connection broken, visionary energy lost.

> —Susan Howe

The recursive might let us don the disguise of "Promethean aspiration: To be a woman and a Pythagorean"—to be a poet hypocrit, and keep "the thread of connection"—"broken lotus root with the fibers still connected"—as inside the wheel of the critical turn we keep researching the curse and walking the desolation high wire.

Recur
4. To come back or return (into, in or to) one's thoughts, mind or memory.

Recurer (obs. rare)
One who helps or aids

Recurrence
Throughout his annual and recurring race he never stops but always changes place; Recurring utterance, a form of aphasia marked by the repetition of certain words or phrases

Recurrent
1597 The muscles which are serviceable to the speech or voice, as are the recurrentes, or retrograding muscles.

Recursant
Of an eagle: Having the back towards the spectator

—O.E.D.

who sing like birds in the pauses of the wind
with their back to the spectator   as a form of address

> I am no doubt not the only one who writes in order to have no face. Do not ask who I am and do not ask me to remain the same: leave it to our bureaucrats and our police to see that our papers are in order. At least spare us their morality when we write.
>
> —Michel Foucault

Dream in which my charge is to write an essay about silence. And so I attempt.
"To speak is to do something."
Or to not speak is to take care. Later, to "speak up" is to "tend"

> Want, Guilt, Need, Care—the four gray hags
>
> —Christa Wolf

To care is the work of the chorus not to express "something outside the action of the play" but to arrest the dialogue without stopping the action in order to reflect or *reflect on* actions. The noise of the *recurrentes or retrograding muscles* in a dance, gestures of utterance issuing from no single character—so, speechless in full speech, masked—on behalf of, to care for, the players in the play, the audience as character in the play—the child at play is in the play

Heart affluence in discursive talk from household fountains never dry

—Thomas Hardy,
definition of discourse, *O.E.D.*

On the waterways the night house becomes a neutrality, not a contested space of subordinates. It apprehends a different relation to the animate objects in its hold—Silently M and I make lists while the children sleep rocking in their bed boats.

The domestic stage, farmyard, feeding place—open air—public:

Behind the closed door a child moved furniture

Written In Furniture

A message arranged
But the recipients unaware of the legibility of this medium

What is it you have come to tell me?

〈XXXXXXX〉

When the angel of death passed over the houses of the Israelites marking doors—dispensing
the pharaoh's rule [as *discursives of moral good and evil, just, unjust*] to some, and sent
(and saved) others under the sign of the bloody X that became wandering in the desert
[*running hither and tither: passing irregularly from one locality to another*], exile, on others—
my forehead—the forehead of my house, received an X. Sent to the lions, the snakes by
the river who secretly romp together disrupting [*passing from premises to conclusions; by
'discourse' of reason; 'ratiocinative'*] the believed order of the nature of animal behavior, I
departed [*running about to the right and the left, laying the separate notices together*]

Here I dwell
and wander

Gather round children of circumstance
while I pass the plate
Let chance, occasion, contingency, condition, happenstance, the circling stars, the odds,
hazard, mistake, incident, be our debtors
          take us hostage
so we have no choice but to pack up and climb out the window
That is to run away, to write, to run back into the burning house

Glory to the combination lock
          with its lost numbers
And the way we look up at story time
thinking the face of the teacher is the book
and our circle the story clock

Come diverge perplex tell ask spoken for speak with quotation, juxtaposition, diagnosis as
proposition—braid doom dwellers, wanderers and the able unable—which dys is it keeping
us doubters, dancers, the aimfully inarticulate, aphasic, estranged, chronically embarrassed,
those who cannot leave the all-you-can-eat smorgasbord, weepers, the exhilarated, army of
archers —Turn, bend, twist, spin, brush-the-knee-and-strike

137

For my pathetic wish to be loved I will substitute a power to love: not an absurd will to love anyone or anything, not identifying myself with the universe, but extracting the pure event which unites me with those whom I love, who await me no more than I await them, since the event also awaits us, *Eventum tantum*. Making an event—however small—is the most delicate thing in the world: the opposite of making a drama or making a story. Loving those who are like this: when they enter a room they are not persons, characters or subjects, but an atmospheric variation, a change of hue, an imperceptible molecule, a discrete population, a fog or a cloud of droplets. Everything has really changed. Great events, too, are made in this way: battle, revolution, life and death…. True Entities are events, not concepts. It is not easy to think in terms of the event. All the harder since thought itself then becomes an event…. ENTITY = EVENT, it is terror, but also great joy.

—Gilles Deleuze and Claire Parnet, *Dialogues*

Coming events cast *light*. It is like dropping everything and walking backwards to something you know is there.

—Dorothy Richardson, *The Tunnel*

◊◊◊◊◊◊◊

NOTES

My Little Read Backwards Book

Previously unpublished.

1. Charles Stein, *Persephone Unveiled: Seeing the Goddess And Freeing Your Soul* (Berkeley, CA: North Atlantic Books, 2006).

Figment of Appointment

Thanks to Kathleen Fraser without whom I may have never encountered Dorothy Richardson's writings.

Previously published in *Chain* 3, Vol. 1, Spring 1996. "Figment of Appointment" is the text of a talk given in November 1994 at Mills College in Oakland, California. It was part of a series called "Mapping a Field of Writing: Poetics Talks *Dialogue* Discussion." The curator of the series, Merle Bachman, wanted poets to read and talk about the writing around, or about, their poetry. Barbara Guest and I titled our evening of talks "Other Lives." Guest had written a biography of H.D., and I had written critically on the work of Dorothy Richardson.

Barbara Guest's biography of the poet Hilda Doolittle is *Herself Defined: The Poet H.D. and Her World* (Garden City, NY: Doubleday and Co., 1984). My work focused on British writer Dorothy Richardson's 13-volume epic novel *Pilgrimage*, published between 1915 and 1935, and her writing on the early silent cinema published between 1927 and 1933 in *Close Up*, H.D., Bryher and McPherson's journal on film (see Susan Gevirtz, *Narrative's Journey: The Fiction and Film Writing of Dorothy Richardson* (New York: Peter Lang Publishing, 1996).

1. Dorothy Richardson, "About Punctuation." *Adelphi* 1.11 (April 1924), 990–996.
2. Richardson, "About Punctuation."
3. Susan Gevirtz, *Linen minus* (Bolinas, CA: Avenue B, 1992). All quotes in Romansh are from Dorothy Richardson.
4. Gevirtz, "Recreative Delights and Spiritual Exercise: Pantheism as Aesthetic Practice in Dorothy Richardson's *Pilgrimage*," *West Coast Line* 26/3 (Winter 1992-93).
5. Richardson, *Honeycomb* (London: Duckworth, 1917), 385. [Richardson's ellipses and

punctuation]; all quotes from Richardson come from novels belonging to the thirteen-volume *Pilgrimage* collection. See **References** for original publication information.

6. Virginia Woolf, "Romance and the Heart: Review of the *Grand Tour*, by Romer Wilson, and *Revolving Lights*, by Dorothy Richardson," *The Nation and Atheneum* (May 19, 1923).

7. Louise Morgan quoted in John Rosenberg, *Dorothy Richardson* (New York: Alfred A. Knopf, 1973), 155.

8. May Sinclair. "The Novels of Dorothy Richardson: Book review of 'Pointed Roofs,' 'Backwater,' 'Honeycomb.'" *The Little Review* 4/12 (1918), 9.

9. Woolf, "Modern Fiction," *The Common Reader, First Series* (New York: Harcourt, 1925), 150.

10. Sinclair, 9.

11. Richardson, "Foreword," *Pilgrimage: Complete in Four Volumes* (New York: Knopf, 1938); reprinted as *Pilgrimage* (London: Virago, 1979), 11.

12. Ibid.

13. Richardson, *The Tunnel*, 13.

14. Richardson, *Pilgrimage*, 12.

15. Richardson, *March Moonlight*, 609.

16. Gevirtz, *Raddle Moon* 11, Vol. 6/ No. 1. (1992).

17. Walter Ong, *Orality and Literacy: The Technologizing of the Word* (London: Routledge, 2002).

18. Gloria Fromm, *Dorothy Richardson: A Biography* (Urbana, IL: University of Illinois Press, 1977), 22.

19. A. Gussow, *A Sense of Place: The Artist and the American Land* (San Francisco: Friends of the Earth, 1973).

20. Roland Barthes, *Empire of Signs*, trans. Richard Howard (New York: Hill and Wang, 1982).

21. Richardson, "Continuous Performance," *Close Up* 1 (July, 1927).

22. Gevirtz, "'Skyey Apparition, White Searchlight': In the Interstices—Dorothy Richardson's Continuous Performance," delivered at the Modern Language Association Conference, New York City, 1992. Paraphrases of sections of this paper appear here.

23. *Dawn's Left Hand* is the tenth novel of the thirteen-novel *Pilgrimage* collection.

24. Richardson, *Dawn's Left Hand*, 217.

25. Sigmund Freud, *Dora: An Analysis of a Case of Hysteria, Volume Four of Collected Papers* (New York: Collier, Macmillan, 1963), 91.

26. Freud, 91-92.

27. Gevirtz, *Prosthesis :: Caesarea* (Elmwood, CT: Potes and Poets Press, 1994).

Dorothy Richardson Taken Place

This is an excerpt from the full text of "Dorothy Richardson Taken Place" published in *Raddle Moon* 11, Vol. 6/No. 1. (1992).

1. Douglas V. Steere, ed., *Quaker Spirituality, Selected Writings* (New York: Paulist Press, 1984), 16–17.

2. Ronald Finucane, *Miracles and Pilgrims: Popular Beliefs in Medieval England* (Totowa, NJ: Rowan and Littlefield, 1977), 63.

3. Stéphane Mallarmé, *Un coup de dés jamais n'abolira le hazard* (A Throw of the Dice will Never Abolish Chance) [1897], in *Collected Poems and Other Verse*, trans. E. H. Blackmore and A. M. Blackmore, (New York: Oxford University Press, 2006), 139.

4. Dorothy Richardson, *Honeycomb*, 489.

Without Event: The Reign of Commotion

Previously published in *A Poetics of Criticism*, edited by Juliana Spahr, Mark Wallace, Kristin Prevallet, and Pam Rehm. (Buffalo: Leave Books, 1994).

ADDRESS

About "The One..." For Asher Montadon

Previously published in "Talks" pamphlet series by Myung Mi Kim, 1991. All were invited to write about the concept of "One."

About About

Previously published in *The Grand Permission: New Writings on Poetics and Motherhood*, Patricia Dienstfrey and Brenda Hillman, eds. (Middletown, CT: Wesleyan University Press, 2003). "Resuscitations" appeared previously in Gevirtz, *Hourglass Transcripts* (Providence, RI: Burning Deck Press, 2001).

1. Rosmarie Waldrop, Introduction to *Paul Celan: Collected Prose*, by Paul Celan, trans. Rosmarie Waldrop (Riverdale-on-Hudson, NY: The Sheep Meadow Press, 1986), viii.
2. Hélène Cixous, *STIGMATA: Escaping Texts*, trans. Eric Prenowitz, Catherine MacGillivray, and Keith Cohen (London: Routledge, 1998), 64.
3. Cixous, 65.

Collision and Forms of Being in Place: *Linen minus, Taken Place*

Previously published in the section titled "Situation: Subject and Position in Poetry" in *Writing From the New Coast: Technique*, *O-blek*, Spring/Fall, 1993.

For Frances Jaffer

Previously published at *HOW2*, http://www.asu.edu/pipercwcenter/how2journal/archive/online_archive, 1999.

1. Frances Jaffer, "February With Chocolates," unpublished poem (dated by Jaffer 4/22/86), n.p. These are the last lines of the poem.
2. Jaffer, "Dictation," *Alternate Endings* (San Francisco: HOW(ever), 1985).
3. Jaffer, "February With Chocolates."

there there: sensation and interruption

Previously unpublished.

Delphic Filmic

Previously unpublished.

Paros Symposium Opening

Previously published at *LRL5*, http://www.littleredleaves.com/LRL5/5home.html
1. See Joseph Mosconi, guest editor, *LRL5*, special feature on the "Paros Translation Symposium," http://www.littleredleaves.com/LRL5/5home.html/. Issue includes translated poetry.

Letter: Translation Panel Invitation

Previously unpublished, this was written in response to an invitation (from Judith Goldman, David Brazil, and Brandon Brown) to participate on a panel about the politics/ethics of translation on August 22, 2007. Invited participants were asked to prepare a 5-10 minute informal talk on their translation practice, "perhaps dilating what you see as the key issues of translation through a discussion of a problem you addressed in translating a specific text."

A Brief Picture Book for Barbara Guest

In memoriam Barbara Guest September 6, 1920 – February 15, 2006

Previously published at *How2*, Vol. 2, No. 4, http://www.asu.edu/pipercwcenter/how2journal/archive/online_archive/v2_4_2006/current/index.htm, 2006.

1. Barbara Guest, "Quill, Solitary *APPARITION*" in *Quill, Solitary* APPARITION (Sausalito, CA: The Post-Apollo Press, 1996), 73.

Orders

Solicited in 2006 for Small Press Traffic's publication *Traffic*, an issue on "Parenting and Writing," that never appeared.

*Epigraph from John Martineau, *A Little Book Of Coincidence: Pattern in the Solar System* (New York: Wooden Books, Walker & Company, 2001).

Doctor Editor

Previously published in *Chain* 1, Spring/Summer, 1994.

1. Elliot George Mishler, *The Discourse of Medicine: Dialectics of Medical Interview* (Norwood, NJ: Ablex Publishing Corporation, 1984), 11.

2. Robert E. Froelich and Marian F. Bishop, *Medical Interviewing, A Programmed Manual,* 2nd ed. (Saint Louis: The C.V. Mosby Company, 1972), 11–12.

3. Helen Flanders Dunbar, *Emotions and Bodily Changes* (New York: Columbia University Press, 1946), 349.

4. Froelich and Bishop, 33–34.

5. Public Enemy, "Cold Lampin With Flavor," *It Takes A Nation Of Million*, produced by Chuck D, Eric Sadler, and Keith Shocklee, Def Jam Recordings/ Columbia CK 44303, CD, 1988.

6. Froelich and Bishop, 57.

7. A.J. Ayer quoted in John L. Coulehan and Marian R. Block, *The Medical Interview: A Primer for Students of the Art,* 5th edition (Philadelphia: F.A. Davis Company, 2006), 71.

8. Mishler, 122.

9. Elizabeth K. Helsinger, Robin Lauterbach Sheets, and William Veeder, eds., *The Woman Question: Society and Literature in Britain and America, 1837-1883, Volume 1: Defining Voices* (New York: Garland, 1983), 16.

10. Charles Bernheimer and Claire Kahane, eds. *In Dora's Case, Freud—Hysteria—Feminism* (New York: Columbia University Press, 1985), 5.

11. Ibid, 1.

12. Ibid, 10-11.

13. See Carolyn Burke, "The New Poetry and the New Woman: Mina Loy," in *Coming to Light: American Women Poets of the Twentieth Century*, ed. D. Middlebrook and M. Yalom (Ann Arbor, MI: University of Michigan Press, 1985), 43-47, 37-57. For background see also Carolyn Burke, "Getting Spliced: Modernism and Sexual Difference," *The American Quarterly* 39/1 (Spring 1987), 98-121.

14. Coulehan and Block, 103.

15. Mishler, 123-24.

16. Ibid, 124.

17. The full citation for the issue reviewed is *HOW(ever)* I/4 (May 1984).

18. Robert Peters, article of unknown origin xeroxed and mailed to *HOW(ever)* office in the period between 1985–1989 (in author's files). Peters, author and editor of the *Peters Black and Blue Guides to Current Literary Magazines*, holds a Ph.D. in Victorian literature and is Professor Emeritus at the University of California, Irvine.

A Place Ajar

Written in response to a query by Susan Smith Nash, editor of *Texture*, to discuss the apocalyptic in one's work. Published in *Texture* 6 (1995), dedicated to this question.

*All quotes or books cited without attribution are by the author: Gevirtz, Susan.
—*Domino: point of entry*. (Buffalo: LEAVE Books, 1992).
—*Linen minus* (Bolinas, CA: Avenue B, 1992).
—*Taken Place* (London, Reality Street: 1993).
—*Prosthesis :: Caesarea* (Elmwood, CT: Potes and Poets, 1994).
Blade Runner. Directed by Ridley Scott, 1982; Warner Brothers, 1994.
Planet of the Apes. Directed by Franklin Schaffner, 1968; 20th Century Fox, 1998.
The Road Warrior. Directed by George Miller, 1981; Warner Brothers, 1982.

Uneven Uneventfulness: Kathleen Fraser's *Discrete Categories Forced into Coupling*

Previously published at *How2*, Vol. 2, No. 4, http://www.asu.edu/pipercwcenter/how2journal/archive/online_archive/v2_4_2006/current/index.htm, 2006.

1. See Burton Hatlen, "Zukofsky As Translator," in *Louis Zukofsky: Man and Poet*, ed. Carroll F. Terrell (Orono, ME: National Poetry Foundation, 1979); see also Kathleen Fraser, *Discrete Categories Forced into Coupling* (Berkeley, CA: Apogee Press, 2004).
2. See Fraser, "*Champs* (fields) & between," in *Discrete Categories Forced into Coupling*. All subsequent Fraser references are from *Discrete Categories*.
3. Hatlen, "Zukosky as Translator," 345.
4. Hatlen, 348.
5. Fraser, "*Champs*," 8.
6. Fraser's italics.
7. Fraser, "You can hear her breathing in the photograph," 48.

8. Fraser, "You can hear," 51.

9. Fraser, "A.D. notebooks," 63.

10. Fraser, "A.D. notebooks," 57.

11. Fraser, "Soft Pages," 21.

12. Chantal Ackerman quoted in Ivone Margulies, *Nothing Happens: Chantal Ackerman's Hyperrealist Everyday* (Durham, NC: Duke University Press, 1996), 4.

13. Fraser, "A.D. notebooks," 66.

14. Fraser, "You can hear," 47.

15. Margulies, 4.

16. Hatlen, 357.

17. Fraser, "*Champs*," 8.

18. Roland Barthes, "From *The Neutral*," October 112 (Spring 2005): 18.

19. Fraser, "You can hear," 49.

20. Fraser, "Soft Pages," 22.

21. Hatlen, 357.

"I like to read in the dark…"

Previously published as part of a "Documentary Survey" for *CHAIN* 2 (December 1994).

Belief's Afterimage: The Recent Work of Barbara Guest

Previously published in *Aufgabe* #1 (2001). Thanks to Myung Mi Kim and Norma Cole, for their readings, and also to John Tranter who invited me to write about Guest's work for his online magazine *Jacket*. An earlier version of this piece appeared at *Jacket* 10, http://jacketmagazine.com/10/gues-by-gevi.html (October 1999). Also, thanks to Vladimir Dzuro, who tracked me after finding his name cited in the online publication, for our ensuing conversation on poetry and forensics.

1. Vladimir Dzuro, Czech Police detective, forensic team, quoted in the *New York Times*, November 1, 1999.

2. Barbara Guest, *Rocks on a Platter, Notes On Literature* (Hanover, NH: Wesleyan University Press, 1999), 3.

3. Barbara Guest, "The Minus Ones," *The Confetti Trees* (Los Angeles: Sun and Moon Press, 1999), 52.

4. σπαραγμός (*sparagmos*): the Dionysian rite of dismemberment performed outside the walls of the polis, usually by women (not citizens) as a holy act. That is, outside of the civil order of the Apollonian governance of the Greek pantheon. Dictionary definition: The tearing to pieces of a live victim, as a bull or a calf, by a band of bacchantes in a Dionysian orgy.

5. Guest, "Nostalgia," *The Confetti Trees*, 14.

6. Guest, "The Minus Ones," *The Confetti Trees*, 52.

7. Martin Heidegger, *Discourse On Thinking*, trans. John Anderson and E. Hans Freund (New York: Harper and Row, 1966), 55.

8. Guest, *Rocks on a Platter*, II, 20.

9. Guest, "Overboard," *The Confetti Trees*, 9.

10. Barbara Guest, "Mysteriously Defining the Mysterious: Byzantine Proposals of Poetry." Excerpts from a talk given by Barbara Guest at St. Mark's Poetry Project (New York City, June, 1986); subsequently published in *HOW(ever)* III (3) (October 1986).

11. Barbara Guest, "Deception," *If So, Tell Me* (London: Reality Street Editions, 1999), 27.

12. Guest, "Doubleness," *If So, Tell Me*, 13.

13. Heidegger, 54.

14. "In Slow Motion," *If So, Tell Me*, 11.

15. Guest, "Details," *The Confetti Trees*, 42-43.

16. Guest, "Deception," *If So, Tell Me*, 26

17. Guest, "annunziare! Dora Films 1913 Elvira Notari in Naples," *If So, Tell Me*, 15.

18. Guest, "Mysteriously Defining the Mysterious."

Errant Alphabet: Notes Toward the Screen

Previously published in *Moving Borders, Three Decades of Innovative Writing By Women*, Mary Margaret Sloan, editor (Jersey City, NJ: Talisman House, 1998).

Motion Picture Home

"Program Notes, *Motion Picture Home*" performed for Poet's Theatre at New Langton Arts, San Francisco, February 9, 2002; excerpt from the play *Motion Picture Home* previously unpublished.

1. Walter Benjamin, "Theatre and Radio: Toward the Mutual Control of Their Work of Instruction," from *Blaetter des Hessischen Landestheaters, Darmstadt*, 1931-32, translated by Louis Kaplan, in *Radiotext(e)*, edited by Neil Strauss, David Mandl, and Bart Plantenga (New York: *Semiotext(e)* 16, 1993), 31.

Outer Event

Published in *Jacket2*, January, 2013, http://jacket2.org.

Thanks to Myung Mi Kim for years of conversation about *Outer Event* and everything else. Thanks also to Nathaniel Tarn whose writings about the choral contributed to my thinking. And thanks to all of those in whose work I first encountered the possibility of something that might be called the recursive: through letter writing (before computers); in the 1987 issue of *ACTS* journal titled "Analytic Lyric"; in the work of Norma Cole; Benjamin Hollander; in Susan Howe's *My Emily Dickinson*; Luce Irigaray; Hélène Cixous; Norman O. Brown's *Love's Body*; Barbara Guest's *Rocks on a Platter*, *Forces Of Imagination*, *Dürer in the Window*, and more recently in the work of Eleni Stecopoulos, Christa Wolf, and Gustaf Sobin, and *Impasse of the Angels* by Stefania Pandolfo. I'm sure there are many more examples unknown to me or forgotten.

Many thanks to George Albon for his invaluable comments on "Outer Event."
Thanks to Martin Inn, t'ai chi teacher, acupuncturist, friend, for comment on this writing and many years of wisdom, healing, and friendship. Thanks beyond possible thanks to Steve Dickison for his repeated readings and indispensible responses to this piece.

*Toni Morrison, *Playing In The Dark: Whiteness and the Literary Imagination* (New York: Vintage, 1993), 4. The full quote is:

> I am interested in what prompts and makes possible this process of entering what one is estranged from—and in what disables the foray, for purposes of fiction, into corners of the consciousness held off and away from the reach of the writer's imagination. My work requires me to think about how free I can be as an African-American woman writer in my genderized, sexualized, wholly racialized world. To think about (and wrestle with) the full

implications of my situation leads me to consider what happens when other writers work in a highly and historically racialized society. For them, as for me, imagining is not merely looking or looking at; nor is it taking oneself intact into the other. It is, for the purposes of the work, *becoming*.

**Michel Foucault, *The Archaeology of Knowledge & The Discourse On Language*, trans. A.M. Sheridan Smith (New York: Vintage, 1982), 215–216. The full quotes are:

Inclination speaks out: 'I don't want to have to enter this risky world of discourse, I want nothing to do with it insofar as it is decisive and final; …All I want is to allow myself to be borne along, within it, and by it, a happy wreck.' Institutions reply: 'But you have nothing to fear from launching out; we're here to show you discourse is within the established order of things… and if it should happen to have a certain power, then it is we, and we alone, who give it that power.' …In a society such as our own we all know the rules of *exclusion*. We all know what is *prohibited*. We know perfectly well that we are not free to say just anything, that we cannot simply speak of anything, when we like or where we like; not just anyone, finally, may speak of just anything.

◇◇◇◇◇◇◇

REFERENCES

Albon, George. *Cafe Tympanum*, one of ten sections from the work-in-progress *Cafe Multiple*. Another section of *Cafe Multiple* was published as *Aspiration* by Omnidawn in 2013.

Barthes, Roland. *Camera Lucida: Reflections on Photography*. Translated by Richard Howard. New York: Hill and Wang, 1981.
—*Empire of Signs*. Translated by Richard Howard. New York: Hill and Wang, 1982.
—"From *The Neutral*." *October* 112, Spring 2005.

Beckett, Samuel. *Proust and Three Dialogues with Georges Duthuit*. London: John Calder, 1965.

Benjamin, Walter. "Theatre and Radio: Toward the Mutual Control of Their Work of Instruction." From *Blaetter des Hessischen Landestheaters, Darmstadt*, 1931-32. Translated by Louis Kaplan. In *Radiotext(e)*. Edited by Neil Strauss, David Mandl and Bart Plantenga. New York: *Semiotext(e)* 16, 1993.

Bernheimer, Charles, and Claire Kahane, eds. *In Dora's Case, Freud—Hysteria—Feminism*. New York: Columbia University Press, 1985.

Blade Runner. Directed by Ridley Scott, 1982; Warner Brothers, 1994.

Blanchot, Maurice. *The Infinite Conversation*. Translated by Susan Hanson. Minneapolis: University of Minnesota Press, 1992.

Brunette, Peter, and David Wills. *Screen/Play: Derrida and Film Theory*. Princeton, NJ: Princeton University Press, 1989.

Bunting, Basil. "The Codex." In *Basil Bunting on Poetry*. Edited by Peter Makin. Baltimore: The Johns Hopkins University Press, 1999.

Burke, Carolyn. "The New Poetry and the New Woman: Mina Loy." In *Coming to Light: American Women Poets of the Twentieth Century*. Edited by D. Middlebrook and M. Yalom. Ann Arbor, MI: University of Michigan Press, 1985.

—"Getting Spliced: Modernism and Sexual Difference." *The American Quarterly* 39/1 (1987), 98-121.

Charcot, J.M. *Clinical Lectures on Certain Diseases of the Nervous System.* Translated by E.P. Hurd, M.D. Detroit: George S. Davis, 1888.

Cheng, Man-ch'ing. *Cheng Tzu's Thirteen Treatises on T'ai Chi Ch'uan,* translated by Benjamin Pang Jeng Lo and Martin Inn. Berkeley, CA: North Atlantic Books, 1985.

Cixous, Hélène. *First Days of the Year.* Translated by Catherine A.F. MacGillivray. Minneapolis: University of Minnesota Press, 1998.
—*STIGMATA: Escaping Texts.* Translated by Eric Prenowitz, Catherine MacGillivray, and Keith Cohen. London: Routledge, 1998.

Cole, Norma. "Why I Am Not A Translator—Take 2," in *To Be At Music: Essays & Talks.* Richmond, CA: Omnidawn, 2010.

Coulehan, John L., and Marian R. Block. *The Medical Interview: A Primer for Students of the Art.* Philadelphia: F.A. Davis Company, 1987.

Deleuze, Gilles, and Claire Parnet. *Dialogues.* Translated by Hugh Tomlinson and Barbara Habberjam. New York: Columbia University Press, 1987.

Derrida, Jacques. "The Double Session." In *Dissemination.* Translated by Barbara Johnson. Chicago: University of Chicago Press, 1981.

Doolittle, Hilda (H.D.). "A Note on Poetry." In *The Oxford Anthology of American Literature,* edited by W. R. Benet and N. H. Pearson. New York: Oxford University Press, 1938.

Dunbar, Helen Flanders. *Emotions and Bodily Changes.* New York: Columbia University Press, 1946.

Duncan, Robert. "Preface" to *Caesar's Gate: Poems, 1949–50*. *Sand Dollar* 8. Berkeley, CA: Sand Dollar Press, 1972.

Engel, George L., and William L. Morgan. *Interviewing the Patient*, 3rd ed. London: Saunders Company Ltd., 1973.

Finucane, Ronald. *Miracles and Pilgrims: Popular Beliefs in Medieval England*. Totowa, NJ: Rowan and Littlefield, 1977.

Fonseca, Isabel. *Bury Me Standing: The Gypsies and Their Journey*. New York: Vintage, 1996.

Foucault, Michel. *The Archaeology of Knowledge & The Discourse On Language*, Translated by A.M. Sheridan Smith, New York: Vintage, 1982.

Fragola, Anthony, and Roch Smith. *The Erotic Dream Machine: Interviews with Alain Robbe-Grillet on His Film*. Carbondale, IL: Southern Illinois University Press, 1992.

Fraser, Kathleen. *Discrete Categories Forced into Coupling*. Berkeley, CA: Apogee Press, 2004.

Freud, Sigmund. *Dora: An Analysis of a Case of Hysteria*. New York: Collier, Macmillan, 1963.

Froelich, Robert E., and Marian F. Bishop. *Medical Interviewing, A Programmed Manual*, 2nd ed. Saint Louis: The C.V. Mosby Company 1972.

Fromm, Gloria. *Dorothy Richardson: A Biography*. Urbana, IL: University of Illinois Press, 1977.

Gaur, Albertine. *A History of Writing*. London: British Library, 1984.

Gevirtz, Susan. "'Skyey Apparition, White Searchlight': In the Interstices—Dorothy Richardson's Continuous Performance," delivered at the Modern Language Association

Conference, New York City, 1992. Paraphrases of sections of this paper appear here.
—*Linen minus*. Bolinas, CA: Avenue B, 1992.

—"Dorothy Richardson Taken Place," *Raddle Moon* 11, Vol. 6/No. 1, 1992.
—"Recreative Delights and Spiritual Exercise: Pantheism as Aesthetic Practice in Dorothy Richardson's *Pilgrimage*." *West Coast Line* 26/3, Winter 1992–93.
—*Taken Place*, London: Reality Street, 1993.
—*Prosthesis :: Caesarea*. Elmwood, CT: Potes and Poets Press, 1994.
—*Narrative's Journey: The Fiction and Film Writing of Dorothy Richardson*, New York: Peter Lang Publishing, 1996.
—*Hourglass Transcripts*. Providence, RI: Burning Deck Press, 2001.

Guest, Barbara. "Mysteriously Defining the Mysterious: Byzantine Proposals of Poetry." Excerpts from a talk given by Barbara Guest at St. Mark's Poetry Project, New York City, June, 1986; subsequently published in *HOW(ever)*, III (3), October 1986.

—*If So, Tell Me*. London: Reality Street Editions, 1999.
—*Rocks on a Platter, Notes On Literature*. Hanove, NH: Wesleyan University Press, 1999.
—*The Confetti Trees*. Los Angeles: Sun and Moon Press, 1999.

Gussow, A. *A Sense of Place: the Artist and the American Land*. San Francisco: Friends of the Earth, 1973.

Hatlen, Burton. "Zukofsky As Translator." In *Louis Zukofsky: Man and Poet*. Edited by Carroll F. Terrell. Orono, ME: National Poetry Foundation, 1979.

Heath, Stephen. *Questions of Cinema*. London: Macmillan, 1981.

Heidegger, Martin. *Discourse On Thinking*. Translated by John Anderson and E. Hans Freund. New York: Harper and Row, 1966.

Helsinger, Elizabeth K., Robin Lauterbach Sheets, and William Veeder, eds. *The Woman Question: Society and Literature in Britain and America, 1837-1883, Volume 1: Defining Voices*. New York: Garland, 1983.

Howe, Susan. *My Emily Dickinson*. Berkeley, CA: North Atlantic Books, 1995.

Jackson, Laura (Riding). First Stanza of "Dear Possible." In *The Poems of Laura Riding, A New Edition of the 1938 Collection*. Edited by Mark Jacobs. New York: Persea Books, 2001.

Jaffer, Frances. *Alternate Endings*. San Francisco: HOW(ever), 1985.
—"February With Chocolates." Unpublished poem, dated 4/22/86 by Jaffer (in author's possession).

Mallarmé, Stéphane. *Un coup de dés jamais n'abolira le hazard* (A Throw of the Dice Will Never Abolish Chance) [1897]. In *Collected Poems and Other Verse*. Translated by E. H. Blackmore and A. M. Blackmore. New York: Oxford University Press, 2006.

Martineau, John. *A Little Book Of Coincidence: Pattern in the Solar System*. New York: Wooden Books, Walker & Company, 2001.

Mishler, Elliot George. *The Discourse of Medicine: Dialectics of Medical Interviews*. Norwood, NJ: Ablex Publishing Corporation, 1984.

Montandon, Asher. Unpublished text (in author's possession).

Morrison, Toni. *Playing In The Dark: Whiteness and the Literary Imagination*. New York: Vintage, 1993.

Ong, Walter. *Orality and Literacy: The Technologizing of the Word*. London and New York: Routledge, 2002.

Peters, Robert. Article from unknown publication xeroxed and mailed to *HOW(ever)* office in the period between 1985–1989 (in author's files).

Planet of the Apes. Directed by Franklin Schaffner, 1968; 20th Century Fox, 1998.

Public Enemy, "Cold Lampin With Flavor." *It Takes a Nation of Million to Hold Us Back*, produced by Chuck D, Eric Sadler, and Keith Shocklee. Def Jam Recordings/Columbia CK 44303, CD, 1988.

Richardson, Dorothy. *Honeycomb*. London: Duckworth, 1917.
—*The Tunnel*. London: Duckworth, 1919.
—*Interim*. London: Duckworth, 1919.
—*Revolving Lights*. London: Duckworth, 1923.
—"About Punctuation." *Adelphi* 1.11 (April 1924): 990-996.
—"Continuous Performance: Almost Persuaded." *Close Up* 1 (July, 1927).
—*Dawn's Left Hand*. London: Duckworth, 1931.
—*Clear Horizon*. London: J. M. Dent and Cresset Press, 1935.
—*Pilgrimage: Complete in Four Volumes*. New York: Knopf, 1938; reprinted as *Pilgrimage*. London: Virago, 1979.
—*March Moonlight*. New York: Alfred Knopf, 1967.
—*Deadlock*. London: Virago, 1979.

The Road Warrior. Directed by George Miller, 1981; Warner Brothers, 1982.

Rodowick, David. "The Figure and the Text." *Diacritics* 15/1 (Spring 1985), 34-50.

Ropars, Marie Claire. "The Graphic in Filmic Writing: *À bout de souffle*, or The Erratic Alphabet." *Enclitic* 5, 2/6, No. 1 (1981-82), 147–61.

Rosenberg, John. *Dorothy Richardson*. New York: Alfred A. Knopf, 1973.

Schivelbusch, Wolfgang. *The Railway Journey: Trains and Travel in the Nineteenth-Century*. Translated by Anselm Hollo. New York: Urizen, 1977.

Showalter, Elaine. *The Female Malady: Women, Madness, and English Culture, 1830-1980*. New York: Penguin, 1985.

Simpson, J.A., and E.S.C. Weiner, eds. *The Compact Edition of the Oxford English Dictionary*. Oxford University Press, 1991.

Sinclair, May. "The Novels of Dorothy Richardson: Book review of 'Pointed Roofs,' 'Backwater,' 'Honeycomb." *The Little Review* 4/12 (1918), 3–11.

Smith, Jonathan Z. *To Take Place: Toward Theory in Ritual.* Chicago: University of Chicago Press, 1987.
Steere, Douglas V., ed. *Quaker Spirituality, Selected Writings.* New York: Paulist Press, 1984.

Stein, Charles. *Persephone Unveiled: Seeing the Goddess And Freeing Your Soul.* Berkeley, CA: North Atlantic Books, 2006.

Stein, Gertrude. "How Writing Is Written." In *The Gender of Modernism*, edited by Bonnie Kime Scott. Bloomington and Indianapolis: Indiana University Press, 1990.

Stewart, Susan. "Letter on Sound." *Close Listening: Poetry and the Performed Word.* Edited by Charles Bernstein. New York: Oxford University Press, 1998.

Tarn, Nathaniel. *Views from the Weaving Mountain: Selected Essays in Poetics & Anthropology, Vol. 1, American Poetry Studies In Twentieth Century Poetics.* Albuquerque: University of New Mexico Press, 1991.

Trinh T. Minh-ha. *Framer Framed.* New York: Routledge, 1992.

Waldrop, Rosmarie. Introduction to *Paul Celan: Collected Prose*, by Paul Celan. Translated by Rosmarie Waldrop. Riverdale-on-Hudson, NY: The Sheep Meadow Press, 1986.

Walter, Eugene Victor. *Placeways: A Theory of the Human Environment.* Chapel Hill, NC: University of North Carolina Press, 1988.

White, Hayden. *The Content of the Form: Narrative Discourse and Historical Representation.* Baltimore: The Johns Hopkins University Press, 1990.

Wolf, Christa. *Cassandra: A Novel and Four Essays.* Translated by Jan van Heurck. New York: Farrar, Straus and Giroux, 1984.

Woolf, Virginia. "Romance and the Heart: Review of the *Grand Tour*, by Romer Wilson, and *Revolving Lights*, by Dorothy Richardson." *The Nation and the Atheneum*, May 19, 1923.

—"Modern Fiction." *The Common Reader, First Series*. New York: Harcourt, 1925.

—"On Not Knowing Greek." *The Common Reader, First Series*. New York: Harcourt, Brace and Company, 1953 [1925].

Wright, Lawrence. "Remembering Satan," Parts I & II, *The New Yorker*, May 17 and May 24, 1993.

NIGHTBOAT BOOKS

Nightboat Books, a nonprofit organization, seeks to develop audiences
for writers whose work resists convention and transcends boundaries.
We publish books rich with poignancy, intelligence, and risk. Please
visit our website, www.nightboat.org, to learn about our titles and
how you can support our future publications.

This book was made possible by grants from The Fund for Poetry and
the Topanga Fund, which is dedicated to promoting the arts and
literature of California.

The following individuals have supported the publication of this book.
We thank them for their generosity and commitment to the mission of
Nightboat Books:

Kazim Ali
Elizabeth Motika
Benjamin Taylor

In addition, this book has been made possible, in part, by a grant
from the New York State Council on the Arts Literature Program.

NYSCA